THE FABULOUS DEMOCRATS

LIBRARY OF CONGRESS COLLECTIONS

THE FABULOUS DEMOCRATS

A history of the Democratic Party in text and pictures

by **David L. Cohn**

with a foreword by The Honorable Sam Rayburn

G. P. Putnam's Sons *New York*

Published on the same day in the Dominion of Canada by Thomas Allen, Ltd., Toronto.

Library of Congress Catalog Card Number: 56-6616

Manufactured in the United States of America

Van Rees Press • New York

Designed by Marilyn Marcus

The author wishes to thank the Library of Congress for its generous help in supplying certain historical data for this book.

The selection from "Bryan, Bryan, Bryan, Bryan" on page 103 is quoted from Vachel Lindsay's Collected Poems, copyright 1925 by Vachel Lindsay, and is used by permission of The Macmillan Company.

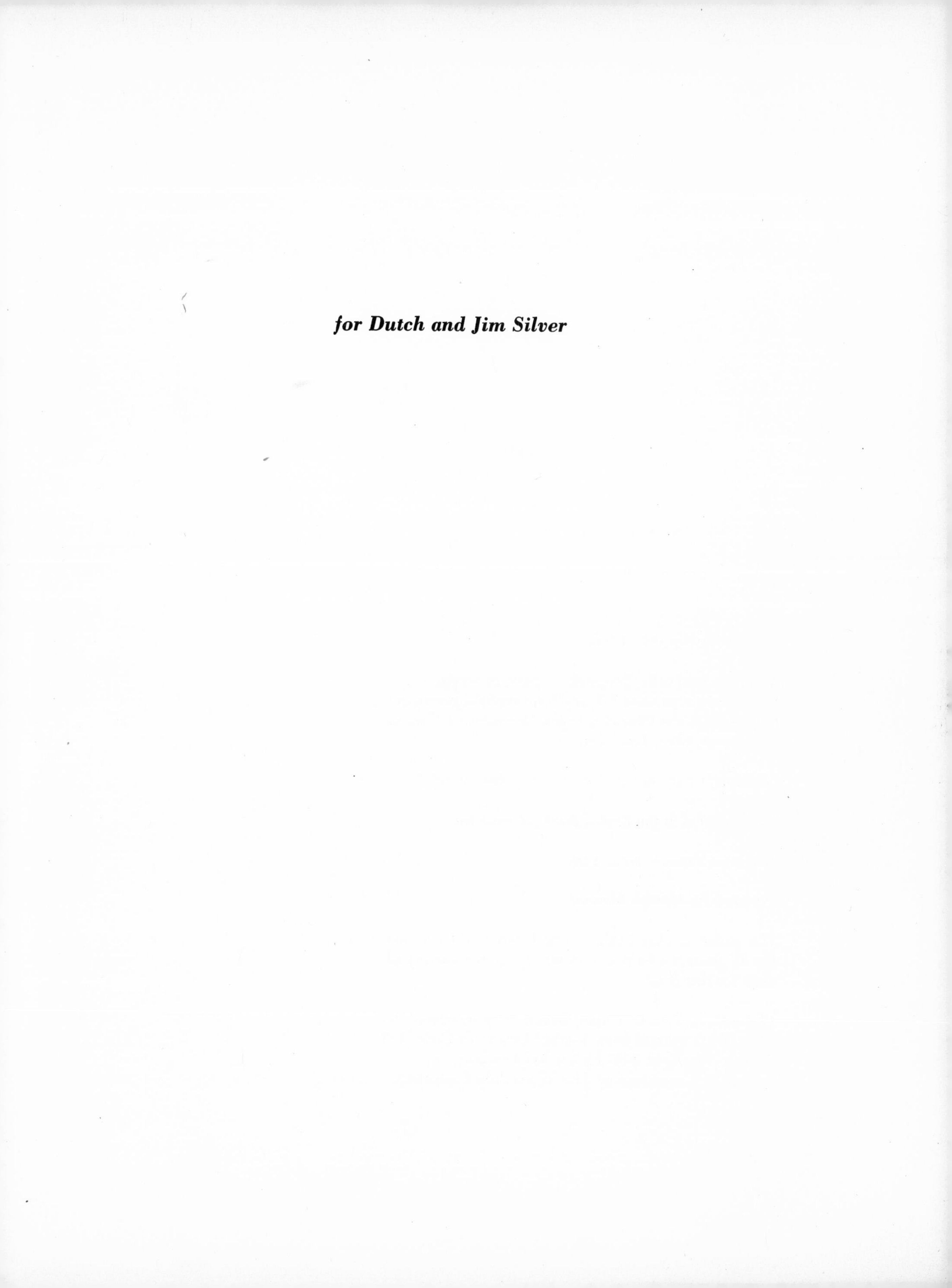

for Dutch and Jim Silver

FOREWORD *by The Honorable Sam Rayburn*

It has been given to me to see much in the long years that the Lord has allotted me, and I have been doubly blessed by being permitted to pass most of my adult life in the public service. I'd like to stop for a moment and say something on this score to my countrymen.

When former President John Quincy Adams announced his intention of running for the House of Representatives, a friend told him that it did not become a former President to seek this less exalted place. Mr. Adams replied that no office in the service of the American people was unworthy of, or unbecoming to, any American. And, as you know, he served in the House and was there stricken with his last illness.

Lord Bryce has noted that democracies, of all forms of government, are most in need of great men. They are also in need of able, devoted men, and never more than now. I hope, then, that many American parents will bring up some of their children—girls and boys—to be public servants as they have long brought them up to be private enterprisers. It is not only that a career in the public service is honorable and rewarding in the most satisfying sense of the word. It is also that if we do not show our love for our country by serving it, some day there may be no country for us to love.

I have read David L. Cohn's book with great interest, and I am glad that while he has at times praised the Democratic party he has also sometimes chastised it, for this is to hew to the line of truth. Yet I believe that a reading of the whole long record of the Party is cause for quiet Democratic pride, and for this reason.

The Democratic party has endured longer than any comparable political institution in the world today. It must therefore have served the people and helped them fulfill their aspirations for a better life on this earth.

Yet we do not ask support for the Party on the ground of its venerability, because there is no inevitable relationship between whiskers and wisdom. The Democratic party retains its high place in American life not because it is old, but because it has a continuing vitality and a continuing adaptability to changing conditions. It is responsive to new ideas. It welcomes experiments. It believes that it is as essential for the prosperity of a political party to improve its "product" as it is for a commercial corporation to improve what it sells. This is not to say, of course, that we are without our share of amiable idiots. But you won't find any old fogies among us. Nor will you find what is still worse—young fogies.

In the fullness of time, then, and of service to the nation, the Democratic party has become more than a political party. It has become an Idea, an essential part of the American Idea. Political parties have their ups and downs. But great ideas go on forever. Hence Democrats look forward with equal serenity to 1956 or 1976.

This is my political belief, and my life has been spent in its service. May I invite you, then, to scan the record as it is briefly set out in this book? Then judge for yourself whether the Democratic party has shown those qualities of wisdom and compassion that make it worthy of the affection and support of the American people.

WORCESTER ART MUSEUM

Life portrait of Thomas Jefferson

The republican is the only form of government which is not eternally at open or secret war with the rights of mankind.

—THOMAS JEFFERSON

1

What is there about Democrats that often sends their opponents into furies of denunciation? Why do they sometimes move their rivals to consume dictionaries of invective as that devouring monster, television, consumes mountains of material? If we try to answer these questions, perhaps we shall achieve some understanding of what the Democratic party was, what it is, and what it hopes to become.

But first—as the commercials have it—let us hear a word from the opposition.

In the summer of 1801, Thomas Jefferson, father of the Democratic party, had been President for a few months. Then, in leafy, summer-drowsy July, there arose the godly Timothy Dwight, president of Yale, who, in the fullness of his wrath, denounced Jeffersonians:

"We have now reached the consummation of democratic blessedness," he said.

"We have a country governed by blockheads and knaves; the ties of marriage with all its felicities are severed and destroyed; our wives and daughters are thrown into the stews; our children cast into the world from the breast and forgotten; filial piety is extinguished, and our surnames, the only mark of distinction among families, are abolished. Can the imagination paint anything more dreadful on this side hell?"

Truth to tell, it could not. And yet. . . One might grant that Jeffersonians were, as the good Timothy charged, "blockheads and knaves." But it is a little hard to believe that they would condemn Federalist ladies of New England to bawdy houses, or tear their babes from them to sell as slaves to the heathen Sultan of Masqat and Oman where they would grow up to become you-know-what.

It was easy for the great cleric to fall into epic denunciation, for he was given to creating majestic effects. In his *The Conquest of Canaan* he set going so many thunderstorms that his friend Trumbull suggested to him that he furnish a lightning rod with each copy of the poem.

The pious churchman denounced Jeffersonians in terms unrelieved by even a smidgen of Christian charity, for two reasons. First, he equated democracy with "immorality." Second, the power of established Congregationalism—almost synonymous with New England Federalism—was faltering. This order, Henry Adams notes, was "a cordial union between the clergy, the magistracy, the bench and bar and respectable society . . ." A ruling class that had created public opinion since early colonial times, it regarded itself as having the right to rule; that indeed "nature" had decreed it should rule. In this sense John Cotton, who wanted the clergy-state, had long ago asked: "If the people be governors, who shall be governed?"

It angered Timothy Dwight that Jeffersonians disputed the "divine" right of Federalists to rule, for to him, upholding the established order—of which he was a pillar and an ornament—was the first of Christian duties, while if the state should fall under control of the godless Jeffersonians, there would be an end to morality and religion.

Dwight, however, was blind to the strong social forces that were beginning to transform the nation, as were many men of his kind. They sought, moreover, simple, black-and-white explanations for the changes that were occurring even if as theologians they often split a hair so fine that the resultant strands were numerous enough to stuff a sofa. Nor is this all. They craved a personal devil upon whom to blame it all. And they found one in the person of Thomas Jefferson.

Yet before continuing our narrative we must clear away some of the confusions of party nomenclature, for as in the beginnings of the republic there were Federalists and Anti-Federalists, later there came to be Republicans and Democrats, with all Republicans claiming to be democrats and all Democrats claiming to be republicans.

Most of the framers of the Constitution looked suspiciously upon political parties. James Madison was fearful that party or, as he said, "faction," might wreck the new republic as it had wrecked ancient republics. It did not occur to him that the Revolution had been made by a party—the "Patriots," the "Whigs"—or that it had its origins in party meetings, that "committees of correspondence" linked party members throughout the states, and that one of the party's Congresses published the Declaration of Independence. So strongly did the Founding Fathers fear political parties that much of the intricate system of checks and balances that they put into the Constitution was designed to prevent the domination of one faction, even if it were like the faction that had brought about the Revolution and written the Constitution. Vice-President John Adams expressed the prevailing opinion when he said:

"There is nothing I dread so much as the division of the Republic into two great parties, each under its leader . . . This . . . is to be feared as the greatest political evil under the Constitution."

But parties nonetheless arose and George Washington was deeply distressed by party divisions soon after he became first President of the new republic. Indeed a bitterly hostile party press rejoiced at his retirement from office and he heard himself assailed, as he complained, "in such exaggerated and indecent terms as could scarcely be applied to a Nero, a notorious defaulter, or even to a common pickpocket."

The presidential elections of 1796 were the first in which Washington was not a candidate, and the third under the new system. Now there could be no doubt that there were two national parties. The Federalists supported John Adams. The Anti-Federalists, or Republicans, supported Thomas Jefferson. Perhaps, however, we may more clearly observe the differences between the parties if we view them through the attitudes of Alexander Hamilton, the Federalist, and Thomas Jefferson, the Republican.

"The Federalists," observes Richard Hofstadter in *The American Political Tradition,* "during Hamilton's service as Secretary of the Treasury had given the government a foundation of unashamed devotion to the mercantile and investing classes. Through his method of funding the national debt, through his national bank, and through all the subsidiary policies of the government, Hamilton subsidized those who invested in manufactures, commerce, and public securities, throwing as much of the tax burden as possible on planters and farmers. . . ."

The Federalist system, whose genius was Hamilton, was a system of centralization in finance, business, and politics. Jefferson had watched it with alarm during the administrations of Washington and Adams, for he believed that the centralization of economic power would destroy "equal rights for all and special privileges for none."

In eighteenth-century America, when it took three weeks to travel from Boston to Philadelphia, Jefferson feared that a strong central government, far removed from the plain people of the country by the endless distances and time-consuming journeys of the day, would fall into the hands of wealthy men, for they alone could manage the outlay required to advance their interests at the distant capital. Once such men controlled the government, they would use it to control the nation's resources for their benefit, and thus economic and political centralization, each aiding the other, would be used to destroy freedom.

Jefferson therefore made economic decentralization his aim. He did so at a time when men believed that property ownership was the source of effective political power, or as John Adams put it, "Power follows property." Jefferson, too, subscribed to this doctrine but he believed in widespread ownership of property as the condition precedent to "equal rights and no special privileges." Hence he preferred an agricultural to an industrial society because widespread ownership of property is easier to bring about and maintain in an agrarian state than in an industrial state.

A Virginia planter himself, and a proponent of an idealistic agrarianism, Jefferson believed that agriculture was the single productive form of labor, and that bankers and manufacturers were members of a class of sterile workers. He believed that government is always at war with natural freedom. The lover of freedom, therefore, will be jealous of delegated power, and will hold the political state strictly to account.

Jefferson sought two great ends: to safeguard freedom from encroachment by the political state, and to establish the rule of justice; and in this search he turned to a laissez-faire agrarianism in opposition to a centralizing capitalism.

"But he was much too sound a political leader and too sagacious a party leader," notes Vernon L. Parrington, "to rest his case upon abstract political theory . . . He kept his mind close to economic fact, and the Jeffersonian movement . . . habituated the . . . electorate to think in economic terms and to regard political parties as the instruments of economic groups . . . A decade of acrimonious debate had made it plain to the common voter that the real struggle . . . lay between the rival capitalist and agrarian interests, of which the Federalist and Republican parties were the political instruments. . . ."

During the first twelve years of the new republic's existence, congressional enactments had made the issues between the groups clearer. The funding plan had increased the numbers and wealth of the rising capitalist group. The coming into being of the first banks and complex credit systems with their hated "paper currency" which drove out the traditional metallic currency, made agrarians fearful and suspicious of the intentions of the moneyed men. A small group in northern cities was growing wealthy from discounting and money brokerage. Farmers and small men, moreover, saw that war had profited the few at the cost of the many; that some of those who had become wealthy through war exploited postwar hardships and grew wealthier from the debts that harassed producing farmers. Now this hitherto negligible but unsleepingly ambitious group turned to the political state as an ally, and under Hamilton's leadership used the central government to serve its financial interests. It was hostile to agrarian programs and had few scruples.

But the landed interests were in a majority and in time they marshalled themselves into a strong party of their own. Then it became the avowed and logical purpose of Jeffersonian Republicans to loose the hands of bankers and manufacturers (Federalists) from the helm of government, and to make the federal government subordinate to the states in all but necessary police powers.

At the risk of great oversimplification, it may be said that the line of division between Jeffersonians and Federalists was not only perhaps between two differing philosophies but also between two kinds of property defined roughly as banking or money property and agrarian or landed property. But nonetheless, neither the Republican party that Jeffersonians called into being, nor the Democratic party that succeeded it, ever abandoned the great end summed up in the words: "Equal rights for all and special privileges for none."

Finally, with respect to party nomenclature, let us turn to that wise commentator on American politics, the British writer D. W. Brogan. He says:

"... By taking the name 'Republican,' the Jeffersonians hoped to pin on their rivals the imputation of being unrepublican. But the Federalists were republicans, although not Democrats." Decades later, "by taking the name Democrats, the majority faction of the Republican party hoped to pin on its foes the imputation of being undemocratic and by the time of the first election of Andrew Jackson, to be deemed 'undemocratic' was almost as fatal in American politics as it is today. By taking the name 'Whig,' the opponents of Jackson hoped to get attributed to themselves some of the aura of revolutionary patriotism that clung about the honored name. And when it was necessary to find some common name for the old Whigs, 'Free Soil' Democrats, desponding 'Know Nothings' who were forced into common action by the introduction of the Kansas-Nebraska bill in 1854, it was soon realized that a mere negative and, possibly, too concrete title like 'Anti-Nebraska,' would not do and the coalition fell back on the sacred name 'Republican,' to show that they, not the slavery-favoring Democrats, were the true heirs of Jefferson. ..."

Since 1868, the two parties have remained the Democratic and the Republican, even if the latter tries to forget the days when it attempted to take over the assets of the Jeffersonians. Yet, as we have pointed out, all Republicans claim to be democrats and all Democrats claim to be republicans, and while this may be clear to Americans it must be bewildering to foreigners who attempt to understand our party system.

* * * *

As the eighteenth century lay a-dying, a sharp class cleavage had arisen in New England. Now Federalists ("nice people") avoided Republicans (Jeffersonians) on the street, and they took their rum at separate taverns.

An almost pathological Federalist hatred of Jefferson, flowing from his advocacy of democratic principles, had pursued him even before he became President in 1800. (He was the nineteenth century's "that man in the White House.") The French Revolution was then strongly in men's minds, as the Russian Revolution is strongly in the minds of this generation. The judicial temperament notwithstanding, Chief Justice Ellsworth in a charge to a Massachusetts grand jury denounced "the French system mongers, from the quintumvirate at Paris to the Vice President [Jefferson] and minority in Congress as apostles of atheism and anarchy, bloodshed and plunder."

(Democrats are still being charged with "atheism." No matter how they may attend church and Wednesday night prayer meetings, go to protracted revivals when crops have been laid by, and tithe for the glory of the Lord, the poor creatures often remain, in Republican eyes, "atheists.")

If Chief Justice Ellsworth's is not a great legal pronouncement, it is an ingenious mingling of the merely vicious with the maliciously injudicious. Yet its only effect was to drive nervous women to hide their Bibles before they could be confiscated by the "atheist" President Jefferson. And since Jefferson, according to Timothy Dwight, was intent upon driving Federalist ladies into lives of shame, theirs would indeed be a fate worse than death. For they would not have even the Bible for comfort in the "stews" to which Jeffersonians had consigned them.

But Mr. Jefferson did not live up to his satanic billing. As Vice-President, he had been living at Conrad's boarding house, and his inauguration was marked by extreme simplicity. Many of his followers indeed had laughed at President Adams' coach and six and American attempts to ape European court ceremonials. Now the President-elect, the first Chief Executive to be inaugurated at the new capital in Washington, walked from his boarding house through the muddy village, surrounded by his followers and drum-beating, flag-carrying militia, to the Capitol. There the oath of office was administered by John Marshall, the recently appointed Federalist Chief Justice.

John Adams, the outgoing President, did not stay for the ceremonies. Early in the morning he left Washington to drive home to Massachusetts. And as he left there passed with him the Federalist régime.

Washington had read his messages to Congress, but Republicans thought that this custom smacked of the King's speech from the throne. Jefferson, moreover, was no orator, and he adopted the practice of sending his recommendations to Congress by a clerk. This remained the unbroken practice of Presidents until 1913, when President Wilson returned to the example set by Washington.

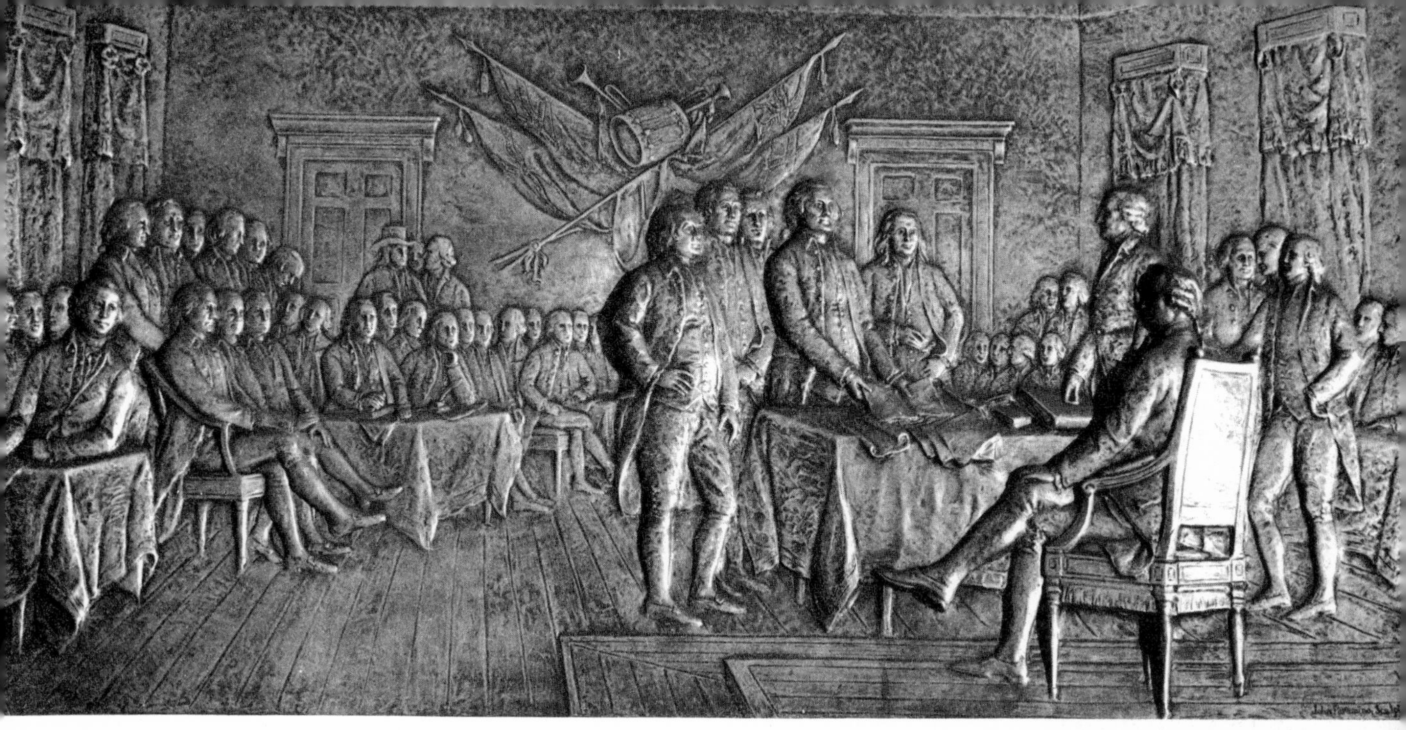

CAMERAMEN, INC.

Authors of the Declaration of Independence report on the work in progress

LIBRARY OF CONGRESS COLLECTIONS

"Millions for Defense"—Jefferson quells Tripolitan pirates

Glorious News!

Republicans Attend---Read---Rejoice !

See what that illustrious President and excellent man, MR. JEFFERSON, has done for us ! All matters in dispute with England are by this time settled—The President has liberated our captive seamen, and by his vigilence and wisdom, will avert war and accomplish all our objects.

The following is from Mr. Lang's Royal Gazette of THIS MORNING.—Read it—read it attentively.

NO TORY.

By the Ship Caledonia, Capt. Henderson, from Liverpool.

LONDON, MARCH 10, 1806.

Several conferences have taken place between Mr. MUNRO, the American ambassador, and his Majesty's Ministers, relative to the matters in dispute between Great Britain and the United States—and there is every prospect of a speedy and amicable adjustment of ALL DIFFERENCES. *Twenty-five American Seamen were discharged on Friday at Portsmouth from the Ville de Milan frigate, Sir R. Laurie, lately returned from the Halifax station. An order we understand has been received to discharge all American subjects from our ships.*

April 30

NEW YORK HISTORICAL SOCIETY

The Last Day.

Every shot's a vote, and every vote kills a TORY !

This is the last day of the election—Shall it close gloriously for Republicans, or in TORY triumph?

Every American will cling to his

COUNTRY ;

Every true whig will oppose with all his might

The Tories ;

Every man in whose veins there runs a drop of republican blood will

SUPPORT THE

Republican Ticket :

He who wishes not this State and the Union to be governed by

British Politics,

Will leave no honorable effort untried to defeat the

British Ticket,

at the head of which stands the name of

RUFUS KING,

The friend of Tory principles—the pander of the British government—the enemy of our republican institutions.

Bad Weather

Will be no excuse for the triumph of a

Bad Cause ;

Every man to his tent, O Israel !

An Old Soldier.

APRIL, 1807.

NEW YORK HISTORICAL SOCIETY

Pro-Jeffersonians twist the British lion's tail

Republicans

Have Never CHANGED their *NAMES:*

Republicans in 1776, *are Republicans yet.*

THE present *American Ticket*---was once the *Federal Ticket*, next the *Federal* Republican Ticket. One hitch more, and it will be right.---The TORY TICKET---then with great propriety they might put a *King* on it.

REPUBLICANS---Be cautious of the golden crown with the flaming eagle upon it---this looks something like "Here you see no liberty cap. "No, this would be against conscience entirely!"

NEW YORK HISTORICAL SOCIETY

Republicans ("Democrats") warn voters to get the genuine article

Jefferson's inaugural address eloquently expressed faith in democracy and republicanism. The election over, "All . . . will bear in mind the sacred principle that, although the will of the majority is in all cases to prevail, that will to be rightful must be reasonable; that the minority possess their equal rights, which equal law must protect, and to violate would be oppression. . . ."

Then nobly Jefferson said:

". . . Every difference of opinion is not a difference of principle. We have called by different names brethren of the same principle. We are all Republicans, we are all Federalists. If there be any among us who would wish to dissolve this Union or change its republican form, let them stand undisturbed as monuments of the safety with which error of opinion may be tolerated where reason is left free to combat it."

The republic was young. It had enemies at home and abroad. Jefferson considered whether the republican United States would endure. He had no doubt that this government, "the world's best hope," would endure, and he said:

"I believe this . . . the strongest government on earth . . . Sometimes it is said that man cannot be trusted with the government of himself. Can he, then, be trusted with the government of others? Or have we found angels in the form of kings to govern him? Let history answer this question.

"Let us, then, with courage and confidence pursue our own Federal and Republican principles, our attachment to union and representative government. . . ."

This classic statement of the democratic faith ranks second perhaps only to Lincoln's Gettysburg Address.

Jefferson's address astonished many Federalists who had expected a violent, inflammatory, partisan utterance. But some remained unconvinced of the President's good faith. (More than a century later, when some Republicans learned—to their relieved surprise—that President Franklin Roosevelt was not going to lop off their heads, they went on believing that he might do so even as they became richer and richer.) Thus Fisher Ames saw himself surrounded by vengeful fanatics in the persons of unoffending Massachusetts Republicans, while the groanings of oxcarts on cobblestones must have seemed to him to presage creakings of overloaded tumbrils taking Federalists to a power-driven guillotine. He was in poor health, but he said that if the Jacobins made haste he "might yet live to be hanged."

Everybody over the age of eighteen understands the meaning of the aphorism, "All that changes is the same." It is also clear that hysteria, if not history, goes on repeating itself. And few of God's creatures are so easily terrified as well-meaning, well-fed, high-church-respectable, upper-tax-bracket conservatives; especially those who are dressed by the best dressmakers of Paris or tailors of London.

Those of the nineteenth century, touched with hysteria as rye bread is touched with caraway seeds, said that Jefferson's doctrines and the doctrines of French revolutionists differed only in the tongue that expressed them. Much later, similar men, caught in the moving stairway of political-economic evolution and unable to go forward or backward, said there was little to distinguish Woodrow Wilson's New Freedom, Theodore Roosevelt's Square Deal, Franklin Roosevelt's New Deal, Harry Truman's Fair Deal, from bloodstained Russian bolshevism. And, they added with mouth-filling tautology, these systems alike espoused "godless atheistic communism."

Perhaps the lesson here is simple: those who mistrust the people, mistrust the elected representatives of the people.

But twentieth-century opponents of democracy are more cagey than their nineteenth-century ancestors. They are also harder to detect because their public relations hirelings have taught them to gild the poison ivy. Federalists perhaps made the political mistake of destroying themselves by frontally attacking democracy. Yet "later enemies of democracy," writes Herbert Agar, "have been wise enough to pose as friends. Often, they have persuaded themselves that they really were friends. And in the shadow of that deception they have fought for the Federalist cause by knifing democracy in the back."

2

Thomas Jefferson, intellectual father of the Democratic party, was not an "average" man—whatever that may mean. He made no attempt to sink to the occasion. Nor did he play down his great qualities and try to convince voters that he was average—"just a simple, humble, Gawd-fearin' man. . . ." (The passion for the average is, incidentally, a masculine aberration. Women, who demonstrably have more sense than men, indulge in no such nonsense. Thus, no woman deliberately tries to make herself plain in order to be regarded as "average." On the contrary . . .) And here we encounter an absurd paradox of today. No farmer, say, is content to own scrub (average) cows, sows, hens, if he can get un-average stock. But he may vote for a mountebank, against a superior man, because the mountebank really is what he says he is—average.

Jefferson, our first great democrat, was erudite. Yet he did not try to conceal his erudition as though it were a secret shame akin to being a sly paregoric drinker. Nor did he manifest an inward contempt for the people by talking to them in pidgin English or in one-syllable words and three-syllable sentences. No public man who trusts the people has two ways of talking: one for his friends in the living room, and another for the public on the platform.

This brings us to another sad little paradox of our times. Most of us have an almost pathetic trust in what we call "education." Believing that it is capable of working miracles, we willingly pay heavy taxes for its sake. But while we trust education, many of us distrust the educated. Hence you may politically destroy a patriot by calling him a "long-haired professor."

There was nothing hawg-and-hominy about Thomas Jefferson even if today some self-styled Jeffersonian Democrats, when running for the offices of Coroner and Ranger, vow their undying love of the Democratic party by equating it with their undying preference for plain vittles, for nothing more high-toned than "'coon and collards."

Such buffoonery, such degradation of the democratic process is, however, no mere joke. Some years ago, a clown from a southern state became Senator because he yawped repeatedly that his opponent, who held the seat, was "up there in Washington City, and while you honest, Gawd-fearin', hard-workin' folks down here are eatin' yo' home-raised ham and eggs, what do you think yo' Senator up yonder is eatin'? Well, I'll tell you! He's eatin' fish-eggs, that's what he's eatin'! Imported, foreign, Rooshian fish-eggs!"

Bilge such as this is, of course, anti-democratic. We take it that what a man eats is his own business. Nor is there any evidence that even a lifetime diet of corn pone and whippoorwill peas ever transmuted a fool into a sage. Jefferson, as it happens, maintained a correspondence with French chefs on the preparation of sauces. Yet he did not fear that his patriotism might be challenged by a political rival asking: "Well, if this feller is such a fine American, how come good, honest American ketchup ain't good for him instead of those highfalutin' imported foreign concoctions he uses?"

Jefferson had a quiet respect for labor. But he expressed it without overwrought, under-documented assertions that "the laboring man is the noblest handiwork of the Lord." (It may be that "God moves in a mysterious way his wonders to perform," but equally mysteriously, thousands of politicians seem to have penetrated the mystery.)

These are some aspects of the man who thought of his election as the "Revolution of 1800." It was, however, scarcely a revolution. It was the expressed recognition of the people that the well-to-do were not born booted and spurred to ride them, and they were not born to be beasts of burden. This meant that democracy was the basis of American life. Federalists failed to understand this. Hence the people voted them into oblivion.

Jefferson bequeathed a cardinal element to the American tradition. It arose from his profound faith in the people; in their ability to decide public matters wisely when *all* the facts of the case were before them.

He trusted the common sense of the people or what he sometimes called their reason. At a time when the European masses were illiterate and were regarded by many of their rulers as an inferior order of human beings, Jefferson said that

Alexander Hamilton, Jefferson's arch enemy and leader of the Federalist party opposition

THE OLD PRINT SHOP

"man was a rational animal, endowed by nature with rights and an innate sense of justice; and that he could be restrained from wrong and protected in right by moderate powers confined to persons of his own choice and held to their duties by dependence on his own will."

Federalist politicians expressed contempt for theories of popular rule. But Jefferson maintained that men "habituated to think for themselves and to follow reason as their guide" could be more safely and easily governed than people "debased by ignorance, intelligence, and oppression." So moved, he said: *"I have sworn upon the altar of God eternal hostility against every form of tyranny over the mind of man."*

Jefferson knew that the people might sometimes be fooled or misled. But he believed that after perhaps many a detour, they would get back on the right path and go straight ahead.

Since this is an important element of the American tradition, democracy, and the Democratic party, it is important to understand, not only what Jefferson believed in this respect, but also what he did *not* believe. Thus some critics of democracy have charged Jefferson with believing that by some mysterious process, some inspiration as of infallibility, there lay in the people a divine source of revelation that led them inevitably to the wisest decisions.

Such nonsense was alien to Jefferson. A child of the Age of Enlightenment, he was given to no form of swami-ism or tea-shoppe mysticism. He exalted the scientific method and extolled reason. He well understood that (in Santayana's words) "scepticism is the chastity of the intellect." Hence he was no unworldly intellectual virgin in danger of being deflowered by the first sweet-talking passer-by.

Jefferson did not commit the Democratic party to the notion that the people are infallible. There was, however, one cardinal thing to which it was committed: the rule of the people. Those who do not trust the people, fear them. Fearing the people, they try to give them little or no share in government, and control them by force or more subtle means. On this score Democrats have fought continuing battles with Republicans.

Jefferson did not believe that men were puppets of the fates and must therefore resign themselves to a bleak stoicism. He thought, on the contrary, that they could strongly affect their destiny on earth. They did not have to sit and "take it," but could improve their condition; and this is the enduring doctrine of Democrats. Jefferson wrote to his friend and political rival, John Adams, about this matter: "... one of the questions ... on which our parties took different sides, was the improvability of the human mind, in science, in ethics, in government, &c. Those who advocated a reform of institutions, *pari passu* with the progress of science [knowledge], maintained that no definite limits could be assigned to progress."

Jefferson was one of the Founding Fathers. But he did not regard them as all-knowing or all-wise. Hence he told Adams: "The enemies of reform ... denied improvement and advocated steady adherence to the principles, practices, and institutions of our fathers which they represented as the consummation of wisdom and the acme of excellence beyond which the human mind could never advance."

(This, however, does not prevent modern political idiots from wrapping themselves in the cloaks of their ancestral betters and mouthing soap-bubble platitudes about "running the country according to the wisdom of the Founding Fathers.")

As Jeffersonians, and subscribers to the doctrine of human change and improvability, Democrats have not believed in bowing to the so-called "God's law of supply and demand," or to any form of human inevitability. The continued differences in this respect between the two great parties came into dramatic focus in the great Depression of the 1930's. Then the Republican Party, because it had failed to mobilize the resources of the country and use them to change the course of events beneficially for all the people, was turned out to pasture by them and there it stayed for nearly twenty years.

Indeed many of the battles fought by Democrats—especially within this century—are parts of continuing struggles that have been in progress for more than a century. Thus, the hullabaloo caused by Franklin D. Roosevelt's so-called "court packing" scheme. Yet as Jefferson grew older, so grew his concern over the Supreme Court, and he constantly reiterated this thesis: "It is a misnomer to call a government republican, in which a branch of the supreme power is independent of the nation."

THE OLD PRINT SHOP

Jefferson buys an empire for $15,000,000

If, he believed, government should be the judge of its own powers, its will might become absolute. Then government's will, not the Constitution, would become the law. "The great object of my fear," said Jefferson, "is the Federal Judiciary." He was fearful of "the consolidation of our government by the noiseless and therefore unalarming instrumentality of the Supreme Court."

Jefferson felt that "It is a very dangerous doctrine to consider the judges as the ultimate arbiters of all constitutional questions. It is one which would place us under the despotism of an oligarchy . . ." Such power was not placed in judges' hands by the Constitution. "The Constitution," Jefferson argued, "has erected no such single tribunal, knowing that to whatever hands confided, with the corruptions of time and party, its members would become despots."

He once called the Supreme Court "sappers and miners" of the Constitution. It was, he felt, undermining the great doctrine of the rights of man. He felt that human rights should take precedence over property rights, but he feared the Constitution would be so interpreted that the rights of man would be overshadowed by an absolute assertion of property. This he took to be the death of the spirit of the constitution.

Jefferson did not win his struggle with the Court, and it continued to interpret the Constitution as the bulwark of property rights. But in 1857 it handed down a decision, logical in terms of its own premises, that shook the country. It was the decision in the Dred Scott case.

The runaway slave, Dred Scott, was captured in a free state. Should he be returned to slavery, or be permitted to remain in freedom?

Scott was a human being. He was also property. How should the Court regard this two-sided man under the Constitution? Should his human side take precedence over his property side? The Court decided that Scott was property. As a Negro, it held, he "had no rights which the white man was bound to respect."

This decision obviously could not be reconciled with the humaneness of the Declaration of Independence, the spiritual charter of the nation. And happily many great Americans who believed that the Declaration is a living document meant to be lived up to by Americans, have continued to quarrel with the Supreme Court because they felt that it was not responsive to its principles. The list, led by Jefferson, includes both Republicans and Democrats: Andrew Jackson, Abraham Lincoln, William Jennings Bryan, Theodore Roosevelt, Franklin D. Roosevelt.

When Jefferson ran for the Presidency again in 1804, the government had achieved a firm place in the affections of the people and its principles were well understood. Voters were therefore not concerned with the kind of government they would have, but only with the question of who would administer it.

Jefferson firmly cemented the nation's democratic government. In the more than sixty years that stretched between his first administration and the Civil War,

LIBRARY OF CONGRESS COLLECTIONS

Two young lawyers—Thomas Jefferson and Patrick Henry

LIBRARY OF CONGRESS COLLECTIONS

The greatest Secretary of the Treasury–Gallatin

NEW YORK HISTORICAL SOCIETY

James Madison,
fourth President of the
United States

the country went through a foreign war and had periods of panic and prosperity. The number of states doubled. The population sextupled. All the while, as is our custom, presidential administrations were assailed bitterly, and men said they were perverting our form of government. But there was never danger of the government's being overthrown by force.

During this time, moreover, secession had been threatened in New England as well as in the South. Yet secession threats testify to the strength and stability of government from which men threaten to secede because it is too strong to be overthrown.

In the years after 1800, thrones and governments constantly fell in Europe. But the United States was becoming as firmly fixed as the enduring hills, one reason for this being that Jefferson's European experience had made him wholly American, and he was our first great leader to construct a political system native to the economics and experience of America.

The Democratic party can rightfully claim to be the child of Jefferson. When it has been at its worst—and it has had periods of shabby mediocrity—it has forgotten Jeffersonian principles. But when it has been at its best, and when it has best served the nation, it has remembered its great patrimony and sought to perpetuate its inheritance in meaningful legislation. At such times it draws much of its inward strength from Jefferson, as it always derives from him its prestige.

3

Jefferson declined re-election after serving two terms as President and thus made the third-term doctrine a part of the unwritten Constitution. If he was the great prophet of democracy, James Madison, his successor in office, has justly been called "the father of the Constitution." He had for eight years been Jefferson's Secretary of State as he had been his first, chief, and well-beloved disciple. Jefferson wrote of him:

"From three and thirty years trial I can say conscientiously that I do not know in the world a man of purer integrity, more dispassionate, disinterested and devoted to pure Republicanism; nor could I in the whole scope of America and Europe point out an abler head."

A man of peace, Madison had to prosecute the somewhat ridiculous War of 1812. At first enthusiastically welcomed, the war was not long supported by the people. Some thought that it was "unrepublican" to levy taxes for war. Bankers and merchants, who generally opposed the war, did not want to lend their money to the government, which had the devil's own time raising funds.

Few wanted to lend money, and fewer still wanted to lend their services. The nation had a population of eight million, but there were never more than thirty-five thousand volunteers at any time, and the war was fought by small numbers of the state militias. Many of their officers were old and frightened, and green troops were ready to leave the battlefield whenever things got tough. The militia would not advance on Montreal, for instance, because it was unwilling to fight outside the United States.

As though this were not enough, the Federalist New England merchants who abhorred the war turned against the Union, called a convention at Hartford, Connecticut, to discuss amendments to the Constitution, and talked about leaving the Union. But in the end they stayed.

Finally, in 1815, the war ended, and January 1, 1816, saw the closing of fifteen years of Republican (Democratic) Administration. The United States had more than doubled its territory since 1800. It was at peace, its ships sailed the seven seas, and it was one of the world's great maritime nations.

James Monroe who, among other offices he had held, had been Madison's Secretary of State, was elected President in a calm campaign. For the first time, an inaugural address was delivered in the open when an "elevated portico" was erected in front of the Capitol, and Monroe addressed a crowd of people, thereby setting a precedent that has been followed to this day.

Now came the famous "era of good feelings." There were controversies over slavery, the tariffs, and internal improvements. But there was peace in the land, business was good, nearly everybody was eating high off the hog, the President was well liked, and the country supported him.

At Monroe's second inaugural, John Quincy Adams wrote in his diary: "The President, attired in a full suit of black broadcloth of somewhat antiquated fashion with shoe- and knee-buckles, rode in a plain carriage with horses and a single colored footman. . . ."

After the ceremonies, Mr. Monroe and friends went to the presidential mansion. It had now been restored and painted white since the British had ravaged it in the War of 1812. "All the world was there," wrote Justice Story. "Hackney coaches, private carriages, foreign ministers and their suites were immediately in motion, and the very ground seemed beaten into powder or paste under the trampling of horses and the rolling of wheels. . . ."

Monroe is best remembered for having laid down the law—the law, so to speak, of the Western Hemisphere—known as the Monroe Doctrine. In a message to Congress on December 2, 1823, he served notice on European autocrats that he would regard "any attempt on their part to extend their system to any portion of this hemisphere as dangerous to our peace and safety." The United States, he said, would not interfere with the colonies in the Western Hemisphere still possessed by European powers. But it would range itself on the side of those who had declared their independence. If any European country tried to oppress or control them, he warned that this would be regarded as "the manifestation of an unfriendly disposition toward the United States."

The Monroe Doctrine, favored by the times and having behind it, in effect, the power of the British Navy, soon achieved an importance in world affairs greater than any that could have been bestowed upon it by the small military might of the rising American republic. No European country, moreover, was in a position to challenge the President's ultimatum, while the Doctrine pleased both Democrats and Federalists. To Democrats it was a vindication of Jefferson's revolutionary principles. To Federalists, it meant that Latin-American ports would be open to their enterprisers.

Monroe left the White House with the plaudits of his countrymen in his ears and without a dime in his pockets. As Jefferson and Madison before him, he retired impoverished from the Presidency.

4

Until the election of 1824, the Democratic party had been unified by the magic of Jefferson's name. Thus in 1816, a majority of the party caucus favored Crawford of Georgia. Jefferson, however, favored Monroe. He won out in the caucus and was overwhelmingly supported in the electoral college against the Federalist candidate, Rufus King.

This method of choosing candidates, unsatisfactory as it was, might have worked so long as Jefferson was present to choose the Presidents. But with his loss of power, or absence, the system would collapse and the party would be torn with struggle.

Under the Constitution, presidential electors were supposed to choose from all available candidates—a system that would have precluded party organization. But almost from the beginning there had been little effort to abide by the Constitution in this respect. It was agreed by tacit consent that electors were figureheads pledged to vote for the candidates of their parties.

In 1824, John Quincy Adams, Crawford, Calhoun, Clay and Jackson sought the nomination. All were supposedly of the Democratic-Republican party, and since the Federalist party was dying, nomination would have been tantamount to election. Jefferson was now ill and no longer attempted to dominate the party, although he preferred Adams over Jackson.

Chaos ruled. No strong man dominated the party. There was no machinery for selecting the party candidate. Four candidates, presumably of the same party, took the field. Supporters of Clay, Jackson, Adams and Calhoun refused to attend the congressional caucus in order to discredit its choice. Whereupon a rump caucus nominated Crawford. At the same time Adams, Clay and Jackson were nominated in mass meetings and by their friends in state legislatures. Calhoun withdrew from the contest and the Adams, Clay and Jackson forces united on him for the Vice-Presidency.

In this political game it was hard to tell which shell contained the pea. There were several candidates and each had a considerable following, but under the Constitution the winning candidate must receive a majority of the votes in the electoral college. Since such a majority could not be attained by any of the contenders, the election was thrown, as constitutionally required, into the House of Representatives. There Clay supported Adams. He became President and John C. Calhoun became Vice-President.

While the vote in the electoral college had been inconclusive, Jackson had the most electoral votes. And now for the first time, estimates were published of the popular vote. According to these Jackson received 150,000 votes, and Adams 114,000.

Jacksonians charged that the people had been deprived of their choice. They said that by a corrupt bargain between Clay and Adams, Clay had used his influence to elect Adams—a charge given color of proof when Adams made Clay his Secretary of State. Jackson accepted the charge as gospel, but proof of it has never been discovered.

It was clear that the Democratic party would have to change, that it must have a more rigid organization. Under Jefferson it had been organized to serve a principle. But its scheme of organization was loose and sketchy, for in the quarter century that had passed since "the revolution of 1800," the party had become a jambalaya composed of all the oddments to be found in the kitchen. It contained Jeffersonians, Hamiltonians, loose and strict constructionists, conservative Federalists desiring tariffs to protect their manufacturing interests, radical frontiersmen seeking a wider application of democracy, slaveholding cotton planters, and New England bankers. As the country's only party, it was of necessity everybody's party.

For a long time only a superficial harmony had marked this discordant group, and even this disappeared in 1824. Hatreds arose between Calhoun and Adams, Jackson and Calhoun, Jackson and Adams, that would long embitter politics and harm the nation. In the struggle that followed the election, Democratic-Republicans split up into two camps. (Jeffersonians were first called Federal-Republicans, then Democratic-Republicans.) Supporters of Clay and Adams became known as National Republicans. But when Andrew Jackson reorganized the Democratic-Republican party, Jacksonians began to call themselves Democrats.

The reorganized, revitalized party was faced with demanding tasks. It had to create an authoritative leadership, and to demand loyalty to it. It also had to exclude all members who were unwilling to proceed on the Party's terms. This being done, there would automatically arise an opposition party, composed of those who would not accept the new leadership of the Democratic party. As for "issues," the opposition would find them as soon as it was given something definite to oppose.

Yet it was not easy to find issues. Jackson, who became the center of the new and rigid group, found them only after the organization was accomplished.

"When Jackson was elected President," writes Herbert Agar, "neither he nor anybody else was certain of what he thought on most of the great issues of the day—banking, internal improvements, slavery, States' rights . . . Jackson was convinced that he ought to be President, knowing that he was a genuine friend of the people and that the people trusted him. So he and his friends built a party machine. The machine made Jackson President. And Jackson then began discovering what he thought about the Bank and allied subjects. As he made his discoveries, one by one, the rebuilt Democratic Party acquired its platform—and the rebuilt opposition acquired its 'issues.' Such a relationship between ideas, and the organization which is supposed to serve the ideas, is not uncommon in history. . . ."

As the new issues emerged, men did not yet clearly understand them, and indeed most of the contemporary leaders had been on both sides of the questions that were presented to the country. Yet as the political machines demanded "regularity" of their members, all, so to speak, fell into place. For now political leaders chose the one side or the other, and they generally abided by their choice.

But before continuing to follow the fortunes of Jackson and the new Democratic party, let us turn back to John Quincy Adams who had become President in 1825.

5

Adams, son of the second President, a high-principled, strong-minded man, had been a Federalist, but in 1808 he had affiliated himself with the Republicans. Scholarly and a professional statesman, he had none of the aspects of the "popular" politician. He said of himself: "I am a man of reserve, cold, austere, and forbidding manners. My political enemies say a gloomy misanthrope; my personal enemies an unsocial savage. With the knowledge of the actual defects of my character, I have not had the pliability to reform it."

Jefferson had supported Adams for the Presidency, and Clay had given him his help. When he became President, it was clear that a new Democratic party machine would have to be built. But who should be the builder? Would it be

Adams and Clay, with Jackson in the opposition? Or would the machine be the handiwork of Jackson, with Clay and Adams in the opposition?

This is not the kind of question that waits long for an answer. Jackson and his supporters immediately began to build foundations for a machine. Adams did not move. His first act indeed, upon becoming President, was to urge a non-party system as the patriotic way. Washington had sought the same end, but it had been shown to be impractical even in the first term of the first President.

The party system is an essential part of the genius of American democracy. The President is not only Chief Executive but leader of his political party. Since, moreover, he is not a constitutional monarch, but must conduct himself as a prime minister in his relations with Congress, he cannot be "above the battle," but only, if he tries hard, above the clouds.

Jackson campaigned against Adams during his entire term. He was assailed as one who had obtained the Presidency by a "corrupt bargain" with Clay. The stern Puritan was even accused, while he had been on an American mission to Russia, of trying to "make use of a beautiful girl to seduce the passions of Emperor Alexander and sway him to political purposes."

Pro-Adams newspapers, in turn, were not shy about Jackson. According to them he was a versatile scoundrel. They said that he was a liar, thief, drunkard, Negro trader, bigamist, adulterer, murderer, cockfighter. He was also pictured as insane, ignorant, cruel, bloodthirsty.

Going beyond even this, they said Jackson had married his wife before she was legally divorced from her first husband, and a pamphlet asked: "Ought a convicted adulteress and her paramour husband to be placed in the highest offices of this free and Christian land?"

Jackson hated Adams because, he felt, the President had permitted Rachel Jackson's name to be dragged into the campaign. He believed that administration slanders had harmed his wife's health, and indeed in one of her last letters Mrs. Jackson said: "The enemies of the Genl have dipt their arrows in wormwood and gall and sped them at me . . . they have Disquieted one that they had no rite to do." Facing death, she wrote that she would rather "be a doorkeeper in the house of God than to live in that palace in Washington."

At his wife's funeral, the mournful, embittered Jackson swore: "In the presence of this dear saint I can and do forgive all my enemies. But those vile wretches who have slandered her must look to God for mercy."

As Jackson worked to win the election of 1828, Old Hickory was presented as the "people's candidate." The Workingman's party in Philadelphia endorsed him. He was supported by eastern workingmen and western farmers. The South was wildly enthusiastic for him. Champion of the "common people," as John Adams had called them, he was the personification of democracy.

By 1828, the country was well on its way toward adult manhood suffrage. The newly enfranchised masses, in a day when the democratic spirit was expanding, believed the time had come to put into action the concept of "Equal rights for all, special privileges for none." The people wanted a more equal distribution of wealth and burdens. They felt that the government should be run by the people, not by a few who ran it for the benefit of a few. And as the practical Jackson men set out, in 1825, to build a new kind of Democratic party, they knew what their task was and how to accomplish it.

First, they must tell the people that Adams had been fraudulently elected. Second, that Jackson was their friend who must be elected in the interest of democracy. Third, every part of the country must be carefully organized by men who would campaign for Jackson throughout the entire Adams Administration.

These objects Jackson men accomplished. Their party kept close contact with the mass of voters through a party press. They held frequent political meetings in every hamlet, town, and city. They reached voters through local clubs and committees headed by job-hungry men who yearned for the trough of federal patronage. They supplied newspapers and the electorate with campaign "literature." In Washington they organized a central correspondence committee that

LIBRARY OF CONGRESS COLLECTIONS

Frontier brawl—Jackson up

LIBRARY OF CONGRESS COLLECTIONS

Jackson becomes a national hero

LIBRARY OF CONGRESS COLLECTIONS

Jackson dismissing the Cabinet

LIBRARY OF CONGRESS COLLECTIONS

A pause for the smugness that refreshes

Politics in the olden time—
General Jackson, President-elect, on his way to Washington

LIBRARY OF CONGRESS COLLECTIONS

Jackson Forever!

The Hero of Two Wars and of Or'eans!

The Man of the People!

HE WHO COULD NOT BARTER NOR BARGAIN FOR THE

PRESIDENCY!

Who, although "*A Military Chieftain,*" valued the purity of Elections and of the Electors, MORE than the Office of PRESIDENT itself! Although the greatest in the gift of his countrymen, and the highest in point of dignity of any in the world,

BECAUSE

It should be derived from the

PEOPLE!

No Gag Laws! No Black Cockades! No Reign of Terror! No Standing Army or Navy Officers, when under the pay of Government, to browbeat, or

KNOCK DOWN

Old Revolutionary Characters, or our Representatives while in the discharge of their duty. To the Polls then, and vote for those who will support

OLD HICKORY

AND THE ELECTORAL LAW.

NEW YORK HISTORICAL SOCIETY

was the forerunner and model for our present national committee. They collected money, printed pamphlets, broadsides and biographies. In short, they did those things that constituted a pattern for future elections.

Jackson was opposed by two-thirds of the newspapers, four-fifths of the preachers, nearly all the manufacturers, and nearly all the banking capital. The richest planters of the Old South preferred Adams to Jackson, even if they had little affection for Adams himself. On Jackson's side were aligned the farmers, especially those burdened with debts and other woes, and the mechanics of the towns who passionately shouted "Hurrah for Jackson!"

The election of 1828 was the first in which the candidates were not selected in congressional caucuses but in big mass meetings. Of the twenty-four states taking part in the contest, in only two were electors appointees of legislatures. In the election, Adams won electoral votes only in New England, and not all of those. Jackson carried the rest of the Union.

"The collapse of the Adams party," wrote Charles A. and Mary R. Beard, "was complete. Gentlemen and grand dames of the old order, like the immigrant nobles and ladies of France fleeing from the sansculottes of Paris, could discover no consolation in their grief."

6

Long before inauguration day, March 4, 1829, Washington was crowded with Jackson's followers. They had come from all over the country to witness the elevation of their hero and, in many cases, to get jobs. Daniel Webster wrote: "I have never seen such a crowd before. Persons have come five hundred miles to see General Jackson, and they really seem to think that the country has been rescued from some dreadful danger."

Jackson walked from Gadsby's, the hotel where he was staying, to the Capitol, followed by shouting, cheering crowds on foot, and by others in wagons and carriages. After the inaugural ceremonies the new President rode horseback down Pennsylvania Avenue to the White House. There, if Webster's word is to be accepted as gospel, men upset punch bowls, broke glasses, and stood in muddy boots on damask chairs to catch a glimpse of their hero. "One hundred and fifty dollar chairs (were) profaned by the feet of clodhoppers." Justice Story of the Supreme Court noted: "I never saw such a mixture. The reign of King Mob seemed triumphant." Mrs. Margaret Bayard Smith, a leader in the local social set, wrote: "The noisy and disorderly rabble . . . brought to my mind descriptions I have read of the mobs of the Tuileries and at Versailles."

As crowds swirled through the White House, friends tried to protect Jackson, who was "sinking into a listless state of exhaustion," from his admirers. Finally, he managed to escape, hurried to Gadsby's, and went to bed, while the punch-drinking celebration on the White House lawn continued for the rest of the night.

Jackson was the nation's first "log cabin" President. Presidents before him came from families of means and cultural accomplishments. All except Washington had been college-educated. None had had to earn a living with his hands. No aristocrat, Jackson was the son of plain, impoverished parents. He had not even been born in the "right" state—Virginia or Massachusetts—but in South Carolina. Still a child when he fought in the Revolutionary War, he was self-taught.

"Emerging as a people's man," wrote Marquis James, "Jackson proferred no ordinary claims to that much-courted distinction . . . He strode forward to inspire, to lead, to govern . . . Andrew Jackson carried his political life in the hollow of his hand, ready to risk it for the cause of the hour whether that cause were great or small, good or bad—the Bank of the United States, the Spoils System, the French indemnity, Margaret Eaton."

His opponents endeared him the more to the people when they sneered at him because, they said, he smoked an evil-smelling pipe, told unprintable stories, "chawed" tobacco, sometimes did not shave for a week. But what was all this contrasted with other things that people heard about Jackson: namely, that he was a regular Bible reader, asked the blessing at the table, and could interminably recite the lines of doleful hymns?

Why did most of the people trust Jackson and admire him? Why did they follow him faithfully? What did he contribute to the Democratic party?

Jefferson and Jackson, so different from one another in so many ways, were alike in this: they were devoted egalitarians. It was an egalitarianism concerned with the rights of small property holders and of individual and free producers. Jefferson, who strove for economic equality, believed that agriculture should be the basis of society; that equal division of inheritances and the ability to acquire lands easily would make for practical equality in status; that universal education would produce accomplished leaders; that immigration should be limited to assimilable stocks and overpopulation avoided, while slavery should be abolished and the slaves transported to a land of their own.

Such a program was acceptable to small farmers, small industrial producers, and mechanics. Andrew Jackson took it over and made it a popular program by making it available to the "humbler members of society" whom he addressed. He knew the aspirations of the people. He shared their hatred of wealth based on speculation and privilege. His public utterances, his prejudices, were harmonious with the spirit of the times.

As Jefferson before him, Jackson declared that the agricultural interest was "superior in importance to all others." He placed himself, he said, at the head of the "humbler members of society—the farmers, mechanics, and laborers who have neither the time nor the means" for looking out for their own rights. And he appeared as the authentic spokesman of the people when he said that a "monied aristocracy of the few" warred against "the Democracy of numbers; the prosperous to make honest laborers hewers of wood and drawers of water to the monied aristocracy of the country through the credit and paper system."

7

As soon as the Jackson Administration had hung up its coat and hat, it began to survey the men who held federal jobs. "No damn rascal who has made use of an office or its profits for the purpose of keeping Mr. Adams in or General Jackson out of power is entitled to the least leniency save that of hanging," wrote one of the President's applicants for a job. "You may say to all our anxious Adamsites that the Barnacles will be scraped clean of the ship of state," declared a member of the Administration. "Most of them have grown so large and stick so tight that the scraping process will doubtless be fatal to them."

This proved to be less terrifying than it sounded, even if one clerk, worried about losing his job, cut his throat, and another went mad. Many of those dismissed from office were found to be scoundrels who were prosecuted and sent to jail for fraudulent transactions while acting as public servants. Numbers of old and faithful civil servants were ousted, but hundreds of others were permitted to retain their jobs despite severe pressures upon Jackson from job-hungry "deserving" Democrats. He was especially reluctant to remove old soldiers from office. When it was proposed that he dismiss the aged postmaster in Albany, he said: "By the Eternal! I will not remove the old man. He carries a pound of British lead in his body."

But it remains true that with whatever moderation Jackson proceeded, he started the custom of making numerous removals of officeholders in favor of party workers, and so gave high sanction to the practice summed up by William L. Marcy, a member of his Administration, in the famous words: "To the victors belong the spoils." The system was decried by intellectuals of Jackson's day and ever since then by politicians who have no opportunity to use it. But it has long since come to be a fixture of our national political life.

It has also long since become a curse to the nation and a national scandal. But the country does little to change it. It submits to it, and blames Jackson for having foisted it upon the country, as though this century-old system could remain "foisted" if the people were really determined to rid themselves of it.

There was, however, more to be done than scraping barnacles from the Ship of State, and Jackson turned to some of the more important issues of the day: the tariff, nullification, the Bank, internal improvements, disposal of the western lands. These questions were primarily economic. Their solution would affect the fortunes of the three great sections of the country: the industrial-capitalistic Northeast, the rural-agricultural-planting South, the farming regions beyond the seaboard and, of course, the great mass of mechanics.

Each section had its champion. Daniel Webster, says Fisher, his biographer, was "the hope and reliance of the moneyed and conservative classes, the merchants, manufacturers, capitalists, and bankers." John C. Calhoun spoke for the southern planters. Thomas Hart Benton was the spokesman of western farmers and land speculators who wanted to get their hands on government lands. Henry Clay, essaying the middle of the road, tried to get the support of both western farmers and eastern capitalists and so reach the Presidency.

Jackson entered the lists as champion of the masses against the moneyed classes. He fought many battles, but here we can concern ourselves only with the struggle over the Bank, and the fight against nullification. The Bank struggle did not end in Jackson's time but, in various guises, has been continued to this day, and is intimately concerned with the story of democracy. The contest over nullification foreshadows the Civil War, and is an essential part of the story of the Democratic party.

In the Bank struggle, Jackson appeared as champion of the "little man" against monopoly, protagonist of the many against the power of Hamiltonian finance, spokesman of the democratic movement that was sweeping much of the nation, and enemy of a powerful institution that was not responsive to the will of the people.

Jefferson had opposed the chartering of the first Bank of the United States because he believed that it would be harmful to the nation, and when its charter expired in 1811, Jeffersonians who were in power did not renew it.

But under Monroe a new Bank of the United States had been chartered for a period of twenty years. Western farmers and eastern mechanics disliked it as a fortress of money power, but also because it would not make unsecured loans to them. Radical Democrats had denounced it on principle from the beginning. It also aroused the anger of state politicians because the Bank's notes, sound everywhere, displaced the shaky currency of state banks that had been chartered by local politicos.

The Bank's managers were charged with showing favoritism to friendly politicians and their backs to Jacksonians trying to borrow money. They were accused of using their currency powers to punish their enemies, bribing congressmen, and spending Bank funds for campaign purposes.

Some charges against the Bank were groundless. Others were justified. Its great Senate spokesman, Daniel Webster, was on its payroll. Once he wrote to Nicholas Biddle, the man who built and controlled the Bank: "I believe my retainer has not been renewed or refreshed as usual. If it be wished that my relation to the bank should be continued, it may be well to send me the usual retainers."

It was also true that the Bank used its power to produce economic distress and crush political opposition. Biddle once told the head of the Boston branch that "nothing but the evidence of suffering abroad will produce any effect in Congress." Webster believed that squeezing the people would be useful to the Bank, and he wrote Biddle that "this discipline . . . must have very great effects on the general question of rechartering the Bank." Indeed the Bank had massed forces for controlling the press, frightening businessmen, defying Jackson and the people. "This worthy President," sneered Biddle, "thinks that because he has scalped Indians and imprisoned Judges, he is to have his way with the Bank. He is mistaken."

Nicholas Biddle, the financial autocrat of his day, had been a child prodigy at the University of Pennsylvania and Princeton, and at eighteen was secretary to the American Minister in Paris. Elegant, suave, a lover of literature, he was a brilliant conversationalist and letter writer. He was also a favorite of fortune, competent, proud, strong-willed. This was the man who now aroused the wrath of Andrew Jackson.

Although the Bank's charter did not expire until 1836, Biddle was anxious to have it renewed so that he could plan for the future; and Clay, looking to the presidential election of 1832, decided to press the matter. Congress, under his leadership, passed a bill granting the Bank's petition for a renewal of its charter.

Jackson vetoed it and called upon the people to support his position. He noted that the people of the western and southwestern states had almost no share in the Bank. They held only $140,000 of the $28,000,000 of capital stock outstanding in private hands. Capitalists of the middle and eastern states held more than $13,000,000. Yet much of the Bank's profits came from westerners.

This meant, said Jacksonians, that the farming West was enriching eastern capitalists whenever it borrowed money. (In later campaigns, "eastern capitalists" have been called by many other names—some of which may not be printed in this family album—such as "Wall Street" and "economic royalists.") Jackson said the "rich and powerful" were using the government for their own private purposes. Nor was this all.

"Many of our rich men," he told the country, "have besought us to make them richer by acts of Congress. By attempting to gratify their desires, we have... arrayed section against section, interest against interest, and man against man, in a fearful commotion which threatens to shake the foundations of our country."

In his famous veto message of the recharter bill for the Bank—described by Biddle as "a manifesto of anarchy, such as Marat and Robespierre might have issued to the mob"—the President stated the social philosophy of the Jacksonian movement.

Although he made it plain that "Equality of talents, of education, or of wealth cannot be produced by human institutions," and that "Distinctions in society will always exist under every just government," he proclaimed that democracy demands on thing—equality of all men before the law, and equal protection by government of all its citizens.

"In the full enjoyment of the gifts of Heaven and the fruits of superior industry, economy, and virtue, every man is equally entitled to protection by law; but when the laws undertake to add to these natural and just advantages artificial distinctions, to grant titles, gratuities, and exclusive privileges, to make the rich richer... the humbler members of society—the farmers, mechanics, and laborers—who have neither the time nor the means of securing like favors to themselves, have the right to complain of the injustice of their Government. There are no necessary evils in government. Its evils exist only in its abuses. If it would confine itself to equal protection, and, as Heaven does its rains, shower its favors alike on the high and the low, the rich and the poor, it would be an unqualified blessing."

This message, striking a new note in American politics, must have seemed to some men of the time—as it did to Biddle—an appeal almost to anarchy. It has caused some men in each succeeding generation to associate the Democratic party with wild-eyed radicalism. Yet it primarily demands nothing more than the realization of the classic democratic ideal—equality before the law, and the restriction of government to equal protection of its citizens. This is obviously the philosophy of a rising middle class. Its object is not to strangle business, but to make certain that the released energies of the people may be fully expressed in creative enterprises. Jacksonians and Jeffersonians were one in their desire to remove government-granted privileges that might impede the workings of the natural economic order.

Jackson knew the people. But his opponents so little understood the country's mood that the Bank published and circulated thousands of copies of the veto message. Then the President simplified the complex, impersonal issue of the Bank, by asking: "Shall the rights of the common man be respected or shall the rich rule the country again?" Who could doubt how the country would respond to this rhetorical question?

Jackson was serene about the action he had taken. "The veto works well," he said. "Instead of crushing me . . . it will crush the Bank." Before the election of 1832 he predicted: "Mr. Clay will not get one electoral vote west of the mountains or south of the Potomac . . ." Events proved him right.

8

The Jackson Administration marks the beginnings of political parties as we have known them for more than a century, and the campaign of 1832 initiated many practices that have since become commonplaces of American politics. Now politicians could no longer achieve their ends merely by conniving with, or conciliating, factions and groups. They had to go to the people. The day of democracy was at hand with all that it portends of good and evil.

As for the Bank, here was a great financial institution ruled by a man of extraordinary force and intelligence, an institution comparable in size to the government itself as a fiscal agency. Issuing one-fourth of the country's bank paper, and having large power over the nation's banks, it was a private agency performing a major public function. But it was almost entirely free of government control. Nicholas Biddle said there were "very few banks which might not have been

LIBRARY OF CONGRESS COLLECTIONS

The heavyweight battle of the century—
Andrew Jackson gets Nicholas Biddle

LIBRARY OF CONGRESS COLLECTIONS

A burlesque of electioneering methods

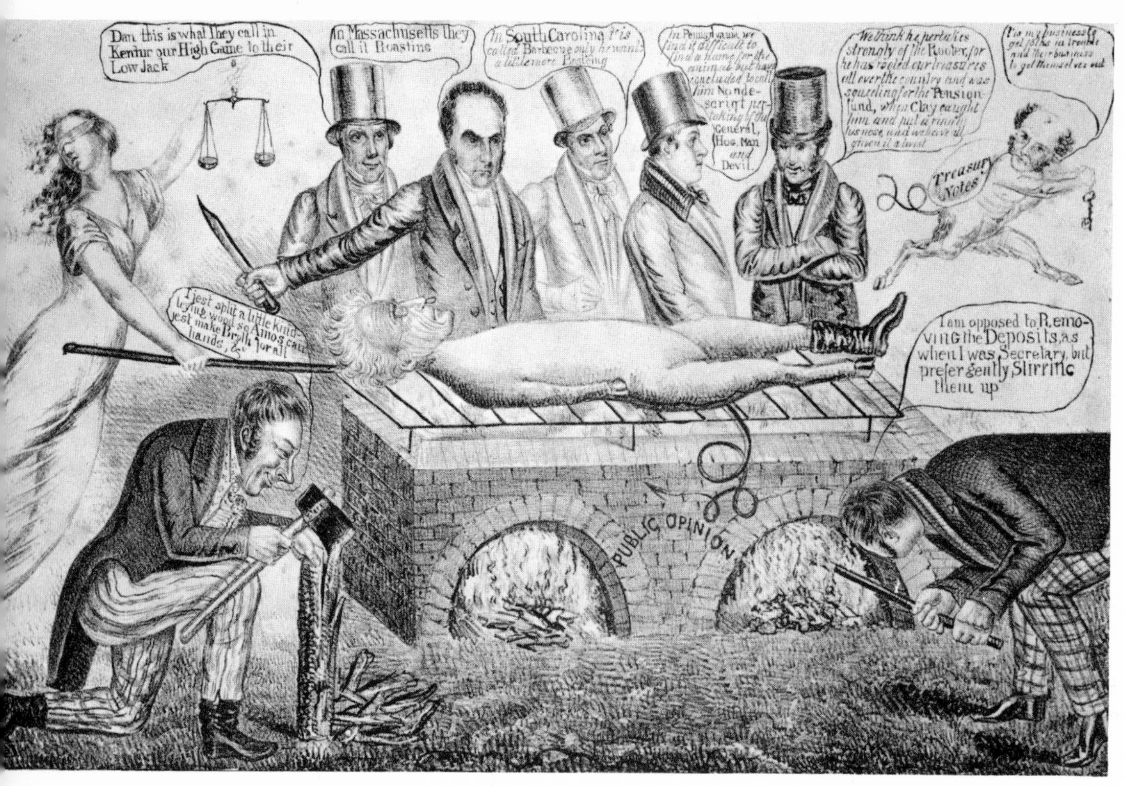

LIBRARY OF CONGRESS COLLECTIONS

Roasting Jackson because of the bank issue

destroyed by an exertion of the powers of the bank." "As to mere power," he wrote, "I have been for years in the daily exercise of more personal authority than any President habitually enjoys." It is not surprising that the Bank's critics saw it as a potential menace to democratic institutions.

There was to come the first of a series of battles that would stretch into the distant future: the "common people" against the "soul-less corporation." This is the heaven of demagogues, and they were out on both sides appealing to class prejudice and class hate; some were for Jackson and some were against him. But the Jacksonians had a greater talent than their opponents for publicity and organization, while they depended on direct appeals to the people to a greater extent than the opposition. The struggle became envenomed and embittered, and Claude Bowers tells us:

"A creature of another world, looking down from the skies upon the United States in the late summer and autumn of 1832, would have concluded that its people moved about in enormous processions on horseback with waving flags, branches and banners. Great meetings were held in groves, addressed by fiery orators, furiously denouncing 'The Monster' and the 'Corporation' and calling upon the people to 'stand by the Hero.' Men left their homes, bade farewell to their families as though enlisting for a war, and rode from one meeting to another for weeks at a time. Nor was this hysterical enthusiasm confined to the more primitive sections of the country. . . ."

For there appeared something else that was new to the political scene: the campaign glee club. Pretty girls sang around hickory poles raised by Jackson idolaters:

> Here's a health to the heroes who fought
> And conquered in Liberty's cause;
> Here's health to Old Andy who could not be bought
> To favor aristocrat laws.

Jackson's powerful personality and measures evoked an enraged, diverse opposition. Capitalists hated him for his Bank policy. Manufacturers disliked his tariff policy. His efforts to rouse "the humble members of society" against "the rich and powerful" disturbed many southerners, and especially planters fearful of the leveling desires of backwoods farmers. South Carolinians sharply opposed him because he had talked of "suppressing insurrection" among them and hanging "traitors."

Jackson's opponents, taking the title Jacksonians had abandoned, at first called themselves "National Republicans," and later "Whigs." In 1832, led by Clay, they tried to oust him from the Presidency. In their ranks were lawyers, merchants, manufacturers, friends of the Bank, businessmen, college professors. The Bank subsidized newspapers through paid advertising. Manufacturers threatened workers with loss of their jobs if Jackson should be elected. A Cincinnati packer told farmers he would pay $2.50 a hundred for pork if Clay were elected, but only $1.50 if Jackson were elected.

Jackson was attacked for impiety. He was accused of the sin of starting a long journey from the Hermitage on Sunday and he appeased the godly only by proving that he had started on Monday. As President, he would not proclaim a day of prayer for relief from cholera, saying that this was for the States to decide. Clay denounced him for "irreligion" and moved a resolution in the Senate to name the day for appealing to God. Obviously a man who advocated "unsound finance" was bound to be an "atheist."

But none of this could defeat the friend of the people and hero of New Orleans. He was elected for a second time by 219 electoral votes as against 49 for Clay.

"Mandate" in hand, he strangled the Bank by withdrawing government funds from it and forbidding further federal deposits in it. In 1836, the second Bank of the United States, its charter expired, automatically came to an end.

Jackson did not relax. He prepared himself for a struggle with Calhoun and nullification.

9

The tariff is perhaps the oldest of American domestic questions. In 1816—with the South's acceptance—the first protective tariff bill was passed. The rates were raised in 1824. In 1828, they were raised again in the "Tariff of Abominations." It led to the emergence of sharply defined sectional differences with respect to protection.

John Calhoun of South Carolina opposed it so strongly that he suggested his state should "nullify" it as unconstitutional. Daniel Webster of Massachusetts strongly favored it.

The men spoke for their communities. The farming South, producer of commercial crops such as cotton and tobacco that were heavily exported, wanted low tariffs. Manufacturing New England wanted high, protective tariffs. This conflict of interest and attitude led to a constitutional crisis and threats of secession.

In 1828, Calhoun wrote *The South Carolina Exposition.* There he made the classic defense of the theory that the States have the right to nullify "unauthorized" federal laws. Senator Hayne of South Carolina defended this position on the Senate floor while the Vice-President, John Calhoun, looked on. If, argued Hayne, the federal government were the judge of its own power, it would be a government of unlimited powers, and the States would be reduced to impotence. It would then follow that one group of people in the country might impose harsh conditions of existence upon the people of another section of the country. And since such a form of government would be unbearable, it could not endure. Hayne said that his state was simply trying to save herself from laws that had severely harmed her economy and would soon wreck the economy of the whole South. And since South Carolina was doing this within the Constitution, she was preserving the federal Union.

Replying to Hayne, Daniel Webster said that the power Hayne would invest in the States belonged to the United States Supreme Court. The Court must decide whether Congress has the power to make any law that it presumes to make. Otherwise the federal government would be a nullity. For one state might accept a federal law, and another might reject it. Webster concluded that nullification is treason, and no state might commit treason without suffering the consequences.

In this great debate, two points of view were put before the nation. Each had merit. Neither could be summarily disposed of by resort to logic or appeal to history. Which point of view would the people support? The answer to this lay largely in the stand Jackson would take.

On April 13, 1830, Jackson and Democratic leaders attended a dinner. All present yearned to know where the President stood on the issue presented in the Webster-Hayne debate. His choice would sharply affect Calhoun's chances for the Presidency as it would also affect interpretation of the Constitution.

During toasts at dinner, Jackson sat impassive, giving no hint of his mind. Finally, he rose. He looked fixedly at Calhoun. He paused briefly. Then he proposed the most dramatic, as it is the most historic, toast in American history:

"Our Federal Union. It must and shall be preserved."

This toast—the equivalent of a presidential proclamation—marked the beginning of the exodus from the Democratic (or Jacksonian) party of the nullifiers and disunionists. Clay would welcome them into the party he was about to create that would do battle with Jackson.

After the toast, the Jackson-Calhoun quarrel grew worse, but the nullification issue would not arise until after the next election.

In November 1832, the South Carolina legislature passed an "Ordinance of Nullification." It declared that neither the "Tariff of Abominations" nor that of 1832 was binding upon South Carolinians. It also passed a law to the effect that if federal officers seized goods for nonpayment of duties, owners of the goods might recover twice their value from the official who seized them. The Governor was authorized to use the militia to enforce the law.

Jackson was scarcely the man to be frightened by a show of force. He nursed, moreover, a consuming hatred for Calhoun, and when he threatened to "hang every leader... of that infatuated people [South Carolina], sir, by martial law, irrespective of his name, or political or social position," no one had to guess at whom he aimed. As news came of South Carolina's action, he prepared the army and navy, and in December 1832 issued his famous Nullification Proclamation. He said he considered "the power to annul a law of the United States, assumed by one State, to be incompatible with the existence of the Union ... and destructive of the great object for which it was founded... Disunion by armed force is treason. Are you really ready to incur its guilt? If you are, on the heads of the instigators of the act be the dreadful consequences."

Strong words, however, did not lead to strong deeds. The country, and Jackson, favored compromise. South Carolina agreed to postpone nullification until Congress should have time to act. Clay put through a bill that lowered the tariff. This pleased the South. But since the reductions would take place only gradually over a ten-year period, protectionists were also pleased. Then the nationalists were placated through a "Force Bill." It gave the President power to use the armed forces to enforce federal laws. South Carolina repealed her Nulli-

LIBRARY OF CONGRESS COLLECTIONS

As Currier saw Andrew Jackson

fication Ordinance. The crisis was over for the time being, but the mighty questions that divided the sections remained unsolved.

Calhoun, at the height of the crisis, had resigned the Vice-Presidency, and in January 1833 he took Robert Hayne's place in the Senate. Soon he joined the Whigs and was warmly welcomed by Clay. In order to be a Whig one had to have only a dislike of Jackson.

At the inauguration of Martin Van Buren as President, Andrew Jackson, debilitated by age and disease, rode with his successor from the White House to the Capitol in a carriage made of wood from the frigate *Constitution*. A great crowd was there, but it was evident that its reverence was for the man who was leaving the Presidency rather than for the man who was entering it. "For once," observed Thomas Hart Benton, "the rising was eclipsed by the setting sun." After the inaugural, as Jackson slowly descended the steps of the portico to his carriage, a pent-up storm of acclamation burst from the throats of the crowd. The cry was such, said Benton, "as power never commanded, nor man in power received. It was affection, gratitude, and admiration . . . the acclaim of posterity breaking from the bosoms of contemporaries."

The following afternoon Jackson walked across the street to the home of Frank Blair for a final visit with the family that had so often given him comforting refuge during his eight stormy years in the White House. He fell into reminiscence. He did not regret crushing the Bank. He did not regret the spoils system. But he did regret that he had never had an opportunity to shoot Clay or hang Calhoun.

Jackson was the nation's first great popular leader. He was its first man of the people. "He was," says Vernon Parrington, "one of our few Presidents whose heart and sympathy were with the plain people, and who clung to the simple faith that government must deal as justly with the poor as with the rich . . . with a courage rare in the White House he dared make a frontal attack on the citadel of exploitation in the face of an army of mercenaries."

At the beginning of the Jacksonian era, Daniel Webster said: "Society is full of excitement: competition comes in place of monopoly; and intelligence and industry ask only for fair play and an open field."

This, despite all the demagogic nonsense hurled at the Jacksonians as enemies of business, accurately expressed the true significance of Jacksonian democracy. The Jacksonian movement, at first a struggle against political privilege, became a struggle against economic privilege. It brought to its side the country's self-made men, rural capitalists and village enterprisers. When, therefore, Jackson left office he was naturally the hero of the lower and middle groups of American society who wanted equal rights in their search for expanding opportunity, and by the time of his death in 1845, his championing of these rights had left a deep and lasting mark upon the country.

LIBRARY OF CONGRESS COLLECTIONS

Old Hickory in old age

"In choosing a party name," writes Parrington, "the Jacksonians were shrewder politicians and better prophets than the Whigs. . . . The American masses . . . had espoused the principle of democracy and interpreted it in terms of political equalitarianism—a principle that had inspired a fanatical hatred in the breasts of old Federalists. To gentlemen of that earlier school democracy had meant the right of the propertyless majority to plunder the minority in the name of the law. . . ."

Whigs avoided this mistake. Instead of denouncing democracy they proclaimed their devotion to it as a vote-getting device. *"They had discovered,"* says Parrington, *"that business has little to fear from a skillfully guided electorate; that the safest way, indeed, to reach into the public purse is to do it in the sacred name of the majority will. . . ."* (Author's italics)

Jackson had long made it known that he wanted his Secretary of State, Martin Van Buren of New York, to succeed him when he left the White House, and he was chosen as the party candidate for the Presidency in the election of 1836.

Jackson declines an admirer's gift of an ornate coffin

LIBRARY OF CONGRESS COLLECTIONS

Death of General Andrew Jackson

LIBRARY OF CONGRESS COLLECTIONS

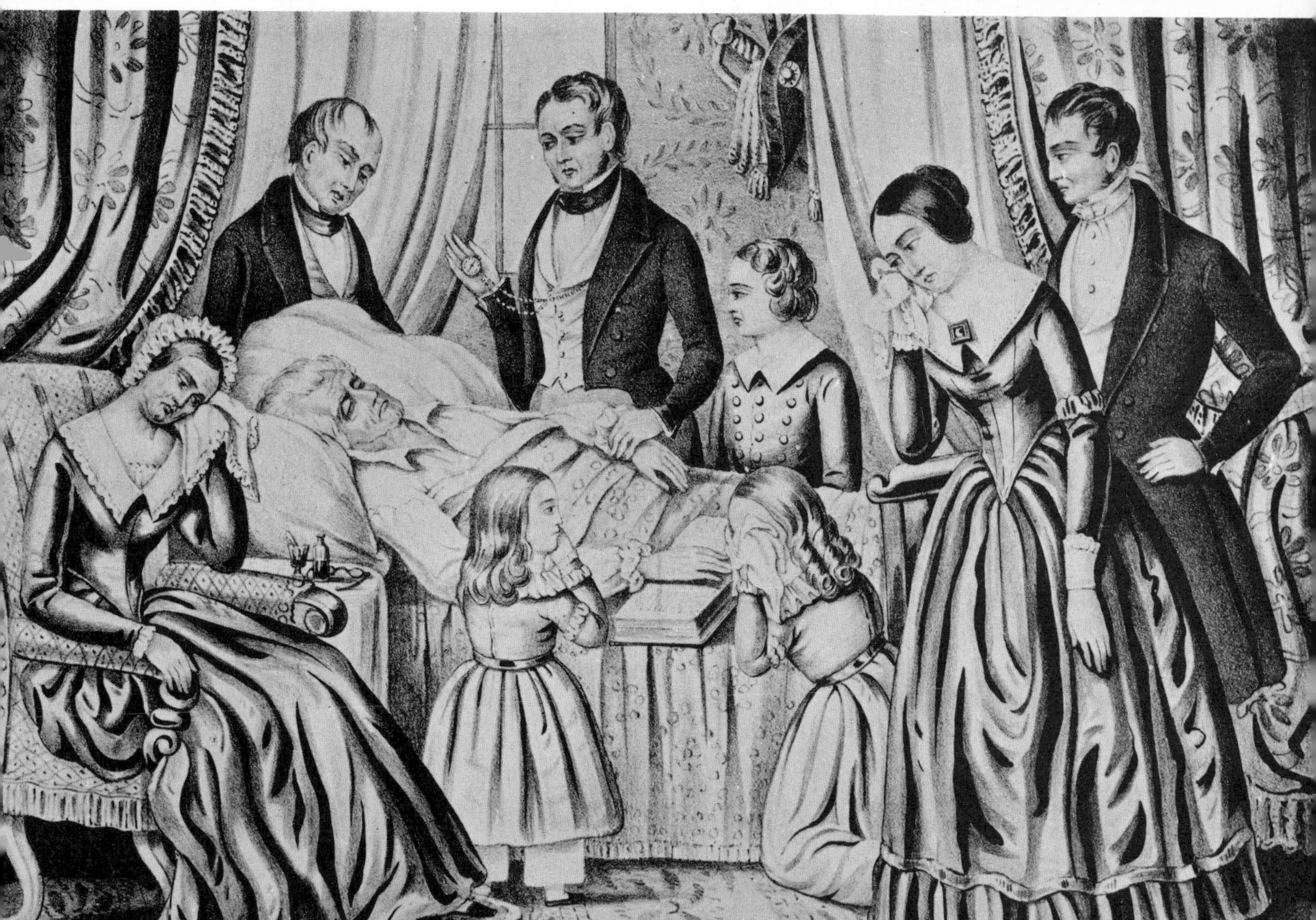

LIBRARY OF CONGRESS COLLECTIONS

The people of New York mourn Andrew Jackson

10

Jacksonians had now discarded the safe label of "Republicans," that had been of Jefferson's choosing, and stood forth as "Democrats." Only a few years before, when a man used that word, he might have had to "smile." But it had now become a household emblem, and those who had once been horrified by it, wore the name with pride.

Whigs chose as their presidental candidate a western farmer and military hero, General William Henry Harrison, whose appeal was the greater to Whig managers because his political opinions, if he had any, were as hazy as an Indian summer dawn. This seemed to qualify him uniquely for the Presidency. The Presidency is the one position for which we seemingly demand neither experience nor knowledge, although we require both of the undertaker even if we shall never need his services again.

Hence the shrewd Biddle told party managers: "If Genl. Harrison is taken up as a candidate . . . let him not say a single word about his principles . . . let him say nothing . . . promise nothing . . . Let no meeting ever extract from him a single word about what he now thinks or will do hereafter."

Who were the Whigs that had chosen such a man? "The Whigs were the party of property and talents," wrote Samuel E. Morison and Henry Steele Commager. "In the North . . . they carried on the nationalist and paternal tradition of Alexander Hamilton. The manufacturing interests which wanted protection, the merchants and bankers who suffered from Jackson's financial vagaries, went Whig. The Anti-Masons, the nativists, and the anti-slavery followers of J. Q. Adams were also absorbed. A large number of Westerners were attracted by . . . the hope of getting something done about the public lands. In the South the Whigs were the party of gentility and property . . . Sugar planters . . . who wanted protection against Cuba; big cotton planters who regretted the veto of the United States Bank . . . ; antique Republicans of Virginia and North Carolina . . . all went Whig. Nowhere but in America could a political party have been formed from such heterogeneous elements."

There were no issues in the campaign. Democrats endorsed Jackson's policies. Whigs denounced Van Buren. Their orators called him a "dandy" who put cologne on his whiskers. Then brewing a storm of mixed, colliding similes, they said he "swaggered like a crow in a gutter," ate from gold plate, and was "laced up in corsets such as women in town wear and if possible tighter than the best of them."

Van Buren was elected, but he had hardly got to the White House when the Panic of 1837 broke over the country. The President took few constructive steps to improve economic conditions, and thus conducted himself within the tradition that would continue into the twentieth century; namely, that the federal government should not undertake the task of restoring prosperity. This task—so the doctrine ran—was one for private individuals.

As the election of 1840 approached, Whigs, seeking a presidential candidate acceptable to the party's improbable membership, again chose William Henry Harrison. Now sixty-eight years old, he was the oldest man ever nominated for the Presidency. For Vice-President John Tyler was chosen.

With Van Buren as Democratic candidate, there began a campaign so nonsensical that, despite the country's capacity for nonsense at all such times, has never been matched. Harrison ("Old Tippecanoe"), remembering Biddle's advice to keep his mouth shut lest a cuckoo fly out of it, opened it only to blame all national woes on Democrats.

President Martin Van Buren

THE NATIONAL ARCHIVES

LIBRARY OF CONGRESS COLLECTIONS

The Panic of 1837 takes over

Harrison was well-to-do. The Whigs were the party of the well-to-do and the well-born. But casting for the votes of farmers and mechanics, they put their campaign on a "po' mouf" basis. Harrison became the "log-cabin and hard-cider candidate." The people were told that he lived in a log cabin, never touched strong liquor, and was a handy man following a plow down a turnrow. Inspired by this demagoguery and determined not to be outdone in the field, Daniel Webster said he would fight any man who accused him of being an aristocrat, and regretted that he had not had the good fortune to be born in a log cabin.

While Whigs made out Harrison, son of a governor of Virginia, to be a log-cabin man, they pictured Van Buren as a Caligula suffering from heartburn caused by eating too-rich foods. They said that he lived in a palace "as splendid as that of the Caesars." The President, they added, slept on French beds and walked on Royal Wilton carpets. But, far worse, not content with simple American fare such as hoghead cheese and turnips, he ate *pâté de foie gras* from silver plates with forks of gold.

Displeased by such infamies in high places, the people threw Mr. Van Buren out of the White House. On inauguration day, the President-elect, the hero of Tippecanoe, Mr. Harrison, rode to the Capitol on a white charger. He took the oath. He delivered a windy address replete with allusions to ancient Rome. A month later he died of pneumonia. He was succeeded by John Tyler, the first Vice-President in our history to become President by succession.

It is worth noting that it was in the campaign of 1840 that the emblem of the rooster and the crow first was used. More precisely it originated in Greenfield, Hancock County, Indiana, around the person of "a famous son," Mr. Joseph Chapman.

Mr. Chapman's tavern in Greenfield was headquarters for the Democrats of that part of the state, and its owner a Democrat of the Jacksonian type, "a man of the people," who served five terms as Representative in the lower house of the legislature. Characterized most notably by his boundless optimism, Chapman habitually at the beginning of each campaign would claim every county in the state, even those most overwhelmingly Whig. To the people of that time this style of electioneering was "crowing." Chapman's style was undoubtedly successful, so much so that he was always sent into doubtful elections to ensure a Democratic victory.

In the 1840 campaign Democrat Van Buren was opposing the Whig Harrison and Tyler ("Tippecanoe and Tyler too") combination with unencouraging results. Alarmed at the report of numbers of Democrats in Hancock County who had bolted to the Whig party, Mr. George Pattison, editor of *The Constitution*, a Democratic paper published in Indianapolis, wrote a letter on June 12, 1840, to the postmaster of the county, and a Democratic leader, William Sebastian. In this letter Mr. Pattison deplores the situation and urges the postmaster to "see Chapman, . . . he must Crow; we have much to crow over."

The phrase, reported in Whig newspapers as "Tell Chapman to crow," gained immediate publicity. The Whigs used it as the butt of their attack, divining correctly the uneasiness of the Democrats in the forthcoming election and their policy of keeping up the fight for the sake of appearance alone. Despite the Whig ridicule, the order "Crow, Chapman, Crow!" with its underlying idea of gameness, daring, or tenacity, caught the popular fancy of the Democrats and they construed it as complimentary to their leader Chapman.

When the Whigs launched their battle cry of "Hard Cider and the Log Cabin," the Democrats, desiring a similar cry, seized upon the phrase "Crow, Chapman, Crow!" and adopted the characteristic fowl, the rooster, for their emblem. Heralded by the Indiana press, the new phrase and emblem gradually received publicity from newspapers of other states, and in a comparatively short time became the recognized national emblem of the Democratic party, supplanting the hickory pole and broom which had been the emblems at the time of Jackson's administration.

It may be added that while the Democratic party was defeated in the national election, Mr. Chapman was re-elected Representative to the Indiana legislature.

The present emblem of the Democratic party, the donkey, may be termed the creation of the eminent cartoonist Thomas Nast. This animal had appeared sporadically in connection with the party, more specifically with Andrew Jackson, but these earlier cartoons were crude in execution and possibly quite unknown to Nast, as they were only posters.

Nast, born in the tiny town of Landau, Germany, in 1840, came to the United States when six years old, settling with his parents in New York City. Rather a disappointment academically, the lad quickly demonstrated his aptitude for drawing, and eventually attempts to induce him to learn music, a trade and to educate him further were abandoned. He became affiliated with *Harper's Weekly*, and played an important role through his cartoons in furthering the political policies of the Republican paper.

It was in the issue of January 15, 1870, that there appeared Nast's first cartoon using the donkey to represent the Democrats. The cartoon, with the caption "A live Jackass kicking a dead lion. And such a lion! and such a Jackass!" portrays a donkey labeled *Copperhead Press* kicking a dead lion, namely Edwin M. Stanton, the Secretary of War who had died only a few weeks before. In thus symbolizing Democratic sentiment, Nast was representing it as the party of noise and obstruction which he considered it to be. He continued to use the donkey to typify the Democratic party when assured by popular acclaim that it had caught the public fancy.

Not until the November 7, 1874, issue of *Harper's Weekly* did the elephant as the symbol of the Republican party appear. In this cartoon, entitled "The Third Term Panic," Nast uses it as a rebuke to a party grown timorous and unwieldy;

different animals of the forest, representing various newspapers and issues, are shown running away frightened from a donkey in a lion's skin labeled Caesarism. The elephant, bearing the inscription "The Republican vote," equally frightened, is bolting toward a pitfall loosely covered with deceptive planks variously labeled as inflation, reform, and so on. Nast continued to draw the elephant in precarious positions indicating the situation of the party at that time.

Gradually both donkey and elephant evolved into generally accepted symbols of the major political parties, and were endowed by them with the virtues they wished them to assume. Thus the Republicans see in the donkey an object of ridicule, stupid and stubborn, whereas the Democrats accept him fondly as a mascot, recognizing that his very humility and homeliness endear him to the people. Likewise the Democrats choose to regard the elephant as a pompous, slow-moving creature, timid, docile, and essentially conservative, whereas the Republicans stress its size, dignity, strength, and intelligence.

Since popular acclaim determines largely the acceptance of party symbols it is impossible to define precisely the time when the donkey superseded the rooster in Democratic affections. One can only note its growing ascendancy, along with the elephant, as a result of Nast's acumen and remarkable skill. It is of interest to note that to this genius the tammany Tiger also owes its creation.

11

Van Buren, Calhoun's rival, to whom Jackson left the Democratic party, represented the northern, big-city Democracy. From 1840 onward it had become increasingly restive because of control of the party by the southern wing. But although Jackson turned the leadership over to a northern man, the North lost control when the country elected Harrison. As the Presidency passed to Tyler, the anti-Jackson, pro-Calhoun wing of the Democratic party began to take over the Whig Administration.

If Harrison had lived, Whigs might have succeeded to a large extent in restoring the Hamiltonian system and re-establishing a third Bank of the United States. But this was not to be with Tyler in the White House. His usefulness on the Whig ticket was that he attracted anti-Jacksonian Democrats in the South. Yet they would not have voted Whig if they had known that the Whigs intended to revive the Bank and interfere with the tariff compromise that South Carolina had won by taking the dangerous step of nullification. If the Whigs had confessed their intentions, Harrison would not have been elected. If Tyler had known of them he would not have gone on the Whig ticket. And his refusal, as President, to bow to heavy pressures, strongly affected American politics.

LIBRARY OF CONGRESS COLLECTIONS

Henry Clay makes a courtesy call on the President. The boys behind the beards have sworn to keep them until Clay becomes President

NEW YORK HISTORICAL SOCIETY

A hostile view of
Martin Van Buren
of Kinderhook, New York

He soon found himself an opposition President, opposed to his Cabinet and his party in Congress. Under Clay's leadership, Congress twice passed bills to revive the Bank of the United States and Tyler twice vetoed them, as he also vetoed two protective tariff bills and another for internal improvements at national expense. This left the entire Whig program in ruins. Clay and Webster, the party's leaders, had outsmarted themselves by their refusal to tell the country in advance what their program was.

Soon the whole Whig Cabinet resigned, except for Webster. Tyler's new Cabinet contained three States' Rights southerners. In 1842 the Democratic party won control of the House of Representatives, Webster resigned as Secretary of State, and Calhoun succeeded him. What was now the score?

In 1840 the Whigs won the national election. But by 1842 there was (in effect) a Democratic President in the White House, a Democratic Secretary of State, and a Democratic majority in the House of Representatives. Nor was this all. The President had vetoed every important piece of Whig legislation.

Democrats had returned to national power and Calhoun and Tyler, returned to the Democratic party, had taken charge of it. Calhoun had long sought to capture the Democratic party for the States' Rights planter group, and to bring leading southerners into it. He had captured the Party. Thereafter, until his death, he sought to persuade southern Whigs that the South could not stand against northern aggression unless southerners united and took leadership of the Democratic party. Southern planters, however, regarded it as corroded with the Jeffersonian doctrine that men are in a real sense equal, and were offended by the concept of "Equal rights for all, special privileges for none." But nonetheless, many great Whig landowners were driven to accept Calhoun's leadership when it became clear to them, in Tyler's administration, that Whigs were committed to the Hamiltonian Bank and Hamiltonian protective tariffs. Lesser southern Whigs came back to the Democratic fold after the Texas question had made slavery a dominant issue.

As the campaign of 1844 drew near, Democrats nominated for the Presidency a friend and neighbor of Andrew Jackson, James K. Polk of Tennessee, the first "dark horse" in the history of presidential elections. Whigs nominated Henry Clay.

Once more the Democratic masses thundered against the "money power." It was worse than ever, they said, and they pointed to Whig efforts to revive the Bank and raise tariffs. But the main plank in the Democratic platform was concerned with Texas. In 1844, Calhoun, as Secretary of State, negotiated a treaty of annexation with Texas, but it was defeated in the Senate. The Democratic slogan became: "All of Oregon, all of Texas." The annexation of Texas, by increasing slave territory, would garner the southern vote. The addition of Oregon to the Union would bring more "free" land to the country and win the

THE NATIONAL ARCHIVES

One of the great
American political thinkers—
John C. Calhoun

How Calhoun looked to the opposition

NEW YORK HISTORICAL SOCIETY

THE NATIONAL ARCHIVES

Henry Clay—the gentleman from Kentucky
who lost the Presidency
by less than 40,000 votes

LIBRARY OF CONGRESS COLLECTIONS

Political commentary was rough in those days

northern vote. Southern planters, alarmed by anti-slavery agitations and profoundly concerned about Texas, began to believe that they would fare better in a democracy of farmers, mechanics, and workers, than with northern Whigs.

Polk was elected President by a small majority. President Tyler, who interpreted the election as a national "mandate" for the immediate annexation of Texas, suggested that Congress pass a joint resolution to that effect. The resolution was passed in February, 1845. A few days later James K. Polk became President and the era of "manifest destiny" opened.

Under Polk, the nation's borders were expanded to the Pacific. He wanted not only Texas, but the vast territory beyond Texas that stretched to the Pacific Ocean, an empire that Polk believed was "destined" to belong to the United States, although it actually belonged to Mexico at the time. A sharply partisan Democrat who thought that no Whig could be a "real" American, pompous, colorless, suspicious, humorless, but fearless, energetic, and independent of mind, Polk became a strong President.

In his administration, the United States added half a million square miles to its territory. He made a treaty with Britain settling the troublesome question of the Oregon boundary. He fought the war with Mexico, the war that Abraham Lincoln

THE NATIONAL ARCHIVES

James K. Polk—a strong president

LIBRARY OF CONGRESS COLLECTIONS

"Manifest Destiny"

thought "unnecessarily and unconstitutionally begun." One of its heroes was General Zachary Taylor.

But while Manifest Destiny was in the air, during the Polk Administration the slavery issue would begin to take its final form and there would appear unmistakable evidences of a drift toward a sectional alignment of the political parties. From now on the Whigs would lose their importance in the South. From now on leadership of the Democratic Party would be in southern hands even though northern Democrats would retain their strength until 1861.

There were now three main groups in the Democratic Party. The first was composed of northern and western agrarians. They disliked slavery, but they did not dislike it enough to go crusading against it. They were Democrats because they favored low tariffs, wanted no Bank of the United States, and liked Jeffersonian democracy.

The second group was composed of northerners from the big cities. The slavery question was a matter of indifference to them. Businessmen among them were Democrats because they wanted low tariffs. Workers among them were Democrats because they were attracted by Jeffersonian-Jacksonian democracy.

The third group was southern and strongly pro-slavery, a group whose leaders were becoming more and more anti-Jeffersonian and anti-democratic.

Northern anti-slavery men regarded the Mexican War as one fought for the benefit of southern, slaveowning annexationists, and abolitionists sought to snatch victory from them through the Wilmot Proviso offered in the House of

LIBRARY OF CONGRESS COLLECTIONS

Inauguration of President Polk—the oath

LIBRARY OF CONGRESS COLLECTIONS

Country's never been the same since

Wishful thinking by Clay's supporters

LIBRARY OF CONGRESS COLLECTIONS

THE OLD PRINT SHOP

News of the Mexican War

Representatives in 1846. It provided that none of the land acquired in the war should be open to slavery. The Proviso was defeated in 1846 and again in 1847. But the country had divided sharply on the slavery issue. Thereafter events would move toward "irrepressible conflict."

As men debated questions raised by the Wilmot Proviso, the Whigs in their nominating convention of 1848 named General Zachary Taylor, hero of the Mexican War, as their presidential candidate, with Millard Fillmore of New York, a lawyer and congressman, as his running mate.

The badly split Whigs issued no platform because they disagreed on basic questions. And the Democratic party was in almost similar estate, principally because the slavery issue transcended party lines.

New York Democrats were divided into opposing factions of "Barnburners" and "Hunkers." Barnburners were strongly anti-slavery. (They were allegedly so fanatical in their desires for reforms that they were likened to the Dutch farmer who burned down his barn to kill the rats.) They approved of the Wilmot Proviso and for their pains the Polk Administration deprived them of federal patronage. The jobs went to Hunkers. (They "hunkered" after jobs.) "Practical politicians," Tammany-supported, they controlled the New York State Democratic convention held at Syracuse in 1847. It rejected a Barnburner resolution opposing the extension of slavery.

LIBRARY OF CONGRESS COLLECTIONS

An anti–Mexican War cartoon

LIBRARY OF CONGRESS COLLECTIONS

General Scott's entrance into Mexico City

The Barnburners bolted the convention and met at Herkimer, New York, in a meeting that was perhaps the first step toward the creation of the Republican party as we know it today. It declared that New York State Democracy would not support any presidential candidate who favored extension of slavery into the territories.

The National Democratic Convention met at Baltimore and chose as its compromise presidential candidate Lewis Cass of Michigan. His opposition to the Wilmot Proviso pleased the South.

Whereupon the displeased Barnburners met at Utica, New York, where they created the Free-Soil Party. Their presidential candidate—a party regular turned maverick—was Martin Van Buren, with Charles Francis Adams, son of John Quincy Adams, for Vice President. The party platform opposed the extension of slavery to the territories.

The Barnburners laid the foundations of the Republican party and at the same time defeated the Democrats in the election, since the Whigs won only because the Democratic vote was split between Cass and Van Buren.

12

The United States had now expanded to the Pacific, and had acquired a huge territory suitable for farming, both in the North and the South. It then appeared that the agricultural interest, exalted by Jefferson and Jackson as the "superior interest," would continue to be the bulwark of Jeffersonian-Jacksonian democracy. And for three decades after the overthrow of John Quincy Adams in 1828, American politics seemed to uphold the Jeffersonian-Jacksonian faith in the struggle against the Hamiltonian system of economy.

"During all these years," wrote Charles A. and Mary R. Beard, in *The Rise of American Civilization*, "the Democratic party won all the presidential elections save two and the exceptions were historical accidents rather than direct defeats on questions of policy. On those two occasions the Whigs . . . made no declaration of principles . . . and swept the polls in the smoke and confusion of a general uproar. Had they confronted the country with a clear-cut program including the bank, the protective tariff . . . it is doubtful whether they could have stampeded the voters into electing either of their martial statesmen."

But as the Whigs became evasive, the Democrats became forthright. They spelled out their 1840 platform so plainly that everybody could understand it. What was it essentially?

It was opposed to the protective tariff, a public debt, the Bank, internal improvements, and interference with domestic institutions of the states. This would remain Democratic gospel until the fateful campaign of 1860.

No effort was made to conceal the nature of the party conflict. In 1848 President Polk in a message to Congress recorded the views of his party. He enumerated Federalist and Whig policies that it opposed—protective tariffs, the Bank, and so forth. He branded them as schemes contrived to transfer money "from the pockets of the people to the favored classes." They revealed a tendency, the President said, "to build up an aristocracy of wealth, to control the masses of society, and monopolize the political power of the country."

How similar are these words of President Polk, uttered in 1848, to those uttered a century later, in 1948, by another Democratic President—Harry S. Truman.

The Whigs succeeded in electing Zachary Taylor, but the victory did little to advance the party's cause. The President, an amiable man and a war hero, did not have any political or economic ideas in his head, and Whigs were silent about principles during the campaign. They elected their candidate but won no popular indorsement of their program; and this victory would be their last victory—at least under the Whig label.

Perhaps Taylor's greatest service in office was not to the country but to literature, and he ought to be remembered for this as well as for the fact that he was father-in-law to Jefferson Davis. "Rotation in office," he once said, "provided good men are appointed, is sound Republican doctrine." This policy caused Nathaniel Hawthorne to be "rotated" out of his place in the Salem customhouse and drove him into writing for a living.

Taylor lived only sixteen months after his inauguration, and was succeeded by Millard Fillmore, who became President on July 9, 1850.

The sectional fight over slavery grew more bitter. It obsessed men. It overshadowed all other questions concerning the nation. The North opposed further extension of slavery. The South, maintaining that slaves were property and therefore protected by the Constitution, insisted that slavery should be permitted on all American soil. Since neither side could prevail, compromise was ordained.

Now came one of the greatest of Congressional debates, the debaters being the giants Henry Clay, John C. Calhoun, and Daniel Webster. Clay spoke for the borderland, Calhoun for the lower South, Webster for the North. All were masters. All were aged. All had given forty years of their lives to the public service. One would die before the debate ended. Another would quickly follow him. And the third—Webster, who appeared stronger than the others—would soon join them in the grave.

Racked by tuberculosis, Henry Clay appealed for compromise as the only alternative to war. When he said that shortly he would lay aside earthly honors and ambitions for the habiliments of the grave, and now cared for nothing except his united country, even the hard-boiled among the audience shed a tear.

Calhoun, who was dying too, was so weak that he had to have his speech read by a friend, while he sat by watching. He explained that the North, through its extraordinary growth, had acquired the power to oppress the South if it chose to use it. He proposed that the South have equal rights in all territories; that the North return fugitive slaves; and that by amendment to the Constitution, equilibrium be restored between the sections.

As the debate raged, Daniel Webster sat silent. Calhoun's speech had been read to the Senate on March 4. Now he came himself to hear Webster's great speech of March 7, 1850, although the shadow of death was upon him. A witness, Peter Harvey, describes the scene:

"Mr. Webster had not been speaking long . . . when I saw a tall, gaunt figure, wrapped in a long black coat, with deep, cavernous black eyes and a thick mass of snow-white hair brushed back from the large brow and falling to the shoulders, advance with slow and feeble steps, through the lobby behind the Vice-President's chair, and then, aided by one of the senators, approach and sink into a chair on the opposite side of the chamber. . . ."

Webster had not seen Calhoun enter the chamber and expressed his regret that the "distinguished senator from South Carolina is prevented by serious illness from being in his seat today."

"At this," says Harvey, "I glanced toward the tall, gaunt figure across the chamber . . . He made an effort as if trying to rise . . . But the effort seemed to be too much for him, for he sank back in his chair evidently exhausted." Webster continued speaking, unconscious of Calhoun's presence, and again expressed his regret that he was absent from the Senate.

Then, says Harvey, "the figure again grew restless; the hands nervously grasped both arms of his chair; the black eyes glared and shone in their eagerness; and now, half rising from his seat and unable any longer to bear the thought that Mr. Webster should remain unconscious of his presence, he exclaimed, in a feeble and hollow voice, which yet was heard throughout the chamber:

" 'The senator from South Carolina is in his seat!'

"Mr. Webster turned toward him with something like a start, and when he saw that his friend had actually risen from the bed of death and had indeed, dared death itself to creep to the Capitol and hear his speech, he for a moment betrayed visible signs of deep emotion. Then, acknowledging his touching compliment by a bow and a smile of profound satisfaction, he went on with his speech.

"A few days more, and Calhoun lay dead, in state, within those very walls."

Webster, to the dismay of the abolitionists, lent his great prestige to compromise on the question of excluding slavery from the new territories, and agreed to a drastic law for the return of fugitive slaves.

In September, 1850, President Fillmore signed a series of bills that constituted the Compromise of 1850. Then a momentarily relieved country turned its attention to the next presidential election.

The Democrats nominated General Franklin Pierce of New Hampshire, son of a New Hampshire governor, lawyer and senator. The Whigs chose as their candidate General Winfield Scott, the sixty-six-year-old hero of the Mexican War. Now there came into play the mudslinging which had become standard practice in presidential campaigns. Mudslinging is, of course, the last refuge of the mentally impotent and the intellectually bankrupt. Thus Whigs called Pierce a drunkard. An Episcopalian, he was charged with anti-Catholicism, while Protestant groups were told that one of his daughters had become a nun. Democrats, in turn, ridiculed Scott because of his nickname, "Old Fuss and Feathers," given him by army officers, and tried to make him appear absurd.

The Democrats won a resounding victory, for Pierce carried every state but four. Particularly notable was the experience of the Free-Soil party in this election. It branded slavery as a crime and demanded its prohibition in the territories. But its presidential candidate, John Parker Hale, received only 156,000 out of more than three million votes.

Democrats at this time seem to have been especially hungry. They were so hungry that Pierce had to ride from Baltimore to Washington in the baggage coach of his train, in order to evade the hordes of ravenous office-seekers who were lying in wait for him. There were so many that numbers of the faithful slept in the rotunda of the Capitol. But come daybreak they were in Lafayette Square, where they looked at the statue of General Jackson, and probably hoped that the new President would have the gumption to kick all officeholders into the street and give their jobs to "deserving" Democrats.

One of Pierce's appointments was particularly happy. The President sent a hungry author as American Consul to Liverpool. His name was Nathaniel Hawthorne.

In the Pierce Cabinet there sat as Secretary of War, Jefferson Davis, who within a few years would be President of the Confederate States of America.

Now that the Whigs were beaten and the Free-Soilers had been put in their place by the electorate, exultant Democrats took over the reins of government, serene in the belief not only that their tenure was secure but that the most violent issues had been "settled." These included the great issues of tariffs for revenue only and slavery. But the party of Hamilton was no little band of abolitionist agitators, and the American political system would soon be shaken to its foundations.

The disturbance began when Congress provided that the territories of Kansas and Nebraska might enter the Union as slave or free states as their citizens should decide. But since these territories lay north of the Missouri Compromise line, the understanding that had long bound the two sections of the country was being set aside. Congress, moreover, declared that the Missouri covenant of 1820 was null and void because it was contrary to the principle of nonintervention on slavery in the territories.

LIBRARY OF CONGRESS COLLECTIONS

Franklin Pierce, who believed that every day in every way . . .

LIBRARY OF CONGRESS COLLECTIONS

General Winfield Scott—"Old Fuss and Feathers"—who lost to General Franklin Pierce

THE NATIONAL ARCHIVES

Jefferson Davis—member of Pierce's Cabinet

The fight over the bill split both Whigs and Democrats into pro- and anti-slavery groups. One result of the fight was that anti-slavery Whigs, Free-Soilers, and Democrats opposed to the Kansas-Nebraska Act, united and at a meeting at Ripon, Wisconsin, in 1854, chose the name "Republican" as the title of their political association.

While Congress heatedly discussed slavery, violence was loosed in the country. John Brown, a man who held that "without the shedding of blood, there is no remission of sins," together with four of his sons, a son-in-law, and two neighbors, raided a pro-slavery settlement near Pottawatomie Creek, in Kansas, and murdered five innocent, unarmed settlers. Nor was the Congress itself free of physical violence. In 1856, Senator Charles Sumner of Massachusetts delivered a powerful oration, "The Crime Against Kansas," that bristled with abuse of the slavery party. But when he made a vehement verbal attack on Senator Butler of South Carolina, Preston Brooks, a representative from South Carolina and a relative of the latter, beat Sumner senseless with a heavy cane as he sat at his desk.

13

The election of 1856 was the first in which the Republicans entered the national field. They nominated for the Presidency John C. Frémont, soldier, explorer, and pathfinder of the West.

Millard Fillmore was the choice of the bigoted, Catholic-hating, foreigner-hating Native Americans or Know-Nothings. A secret party, when members were asked about their political beliefs, they answered "I know nothing;" hence the name "Know-Nothings."

The Democrats chose James Buchanan of Pennsylvania as their presidential candidate, in part for the reason that he had been Minister to Great Britain during the Kansas-Nebraska debates and was not a party to either side of the controversy.

The Republican slogan was "Free soil, free speech, and Frémont." The party's most important plank declared that it was the duty of Congress to prohibit in the territories "those twin relics of barbarism—polygamy and slavery."

The Democratic platform, aside from declaring that "the party will resist all attempts at renewing . . . the agitation of the slavery question . . ." made it clear that it was opposed to secret political parties whose members held themselves out to be what we should now call "one hundred per cent Americans."

The Democratic party resolved that the foundation of the United States was built upon "entire freedom in matters of religious concernment, and no respect of persons in regard to . . . place of birth." Hence a "political crusade . . . against Catholics and foreign-born" is not "in unison with the spirit of . . . enlightened freedom which distinguishes the American system of popular government."

THE NATIONAL ARCHIVES

James Buchanan—our only bachelor President

LIBRARY OF CONGRESS COLLECTIONS

The bachelor President's official hostess—
his niece, Harriet Lane

LIBRARY OF CONGRESS COLLECTIONS

Politicking was fun before television came

LIBRARY OF CONGRESS COLLECTIONS

Buchanan was inaugurated

just in time for the Panic of 1857

LIBRARY OF CONGRESS COLLECTIONS

The issue of the campaign was "bleeding Kansas." Its distinguishing feature perhaps was the high quota of literacy that was brought to bear by the new party, the Republicans. In this day of "progress" when it is thought by many that reading poetry is "unmanly," while to write it is to make one's "manliness" suspect, the Republicans brought up as campaign orators two poets—William Cullen Bryant and Henry Wadsworth Longfellow. They also had a speaker who had made a good name for himself as a lecturer, poet, and essayist. His name was Ralph Waldo Emerson.

Query: Would either of the great political parties in this day of universal "education" enlist as party speakers men such as Robert Frost or William Faulkner?

But to return to the campaign of 1856. Buchanan won the election with 1,838,169 popular votes against Frémont's 1,341,264 and Fillmore's 874,534.

The country drifted toward disunion. The sixty-six-year-old bachelor President had been in office only two days when the country was shaken by the Dred Scott decision of the Supreme Court. It held that the Missouri Compromise was unconstitutional, that a slave was property, and that Congress could no more exclude such property from a territory than it could any other.

In 1858 the country's attention became centered upon a series of debates in Illinois between Abraham Lincoln, a Springfield, Illinois, lawyer and former congressman, and Stephen A. Douglas, a Democratic senator from Illinois. The debates clearly defined the conflicting programs for excluding slavery from the territories and the squatter-sovereignty scheme for letting the inhabitants decide for themselves.

In 1859 there came the appalling act of John Brown. In the spring of that year, after attending an anti-slavery convention, he muttered: "These men are all talk; what we need is action—action!" Soon he and a few comrades made a raid into Harper's Ferry, Virginia, for the purpose of starting a slave uprising throughout the South. He failed and was executed as a "traitor to Virginia," but his act of violence rocked the nation from coast to coast.

And seven years before this time, in 1852, there had been published Harriet Beecher Stowe's *Uncle Tom's Cabin.* The most widely read book of its day, though it was practically excluded from the South, it deeply moved men and women who had never read a serious book about slavery or heard a serious discussion of the question.

The fears and turmoil of the country were echoed in Congress. There reason gave way to unreason, logic to passion, passion to verbal and physical violence, while sectional animosity was increased by events in Kansas, to which Buchanan had sent a pro-slavery governor.

The Panic of 1857 and the President's pro-slavery attitudes drove many voters from Democratic ranks. Industrialists who wanted protective tariffs, bankers desiring an improved banking system, and westerners hankering for free public

LIBRARY OF CONGRESS COLLECTIONS

Sleeping room of the northwestern delegation,
Hibernian Hall, Charleston. Devotion above and beyond . . .

LIBRARY OF CONGRESS COLLECTIONS

Stephen A. Douglas,
who debated the issue of slavery
with a Springfield, Illinois, lawyer

lands, turned Republican. The nation seemed to be approaching a state of anarchy as southern congressmen voted against measures that would benefit the North, and northern congressmen, retaliating, made the Fugitive Slave Law a dead letter.

In April 1860, when the Democratic nominating convention assembled in Charleston—the center of pro-slavery sentiments—division among Democrats was sharp. Northern Democrats were unwilling to go along with the South by commending slavery and saying that it ought to be made obligatory in the territories. Nor would they attempt to guarantee the planters sovereignty in the party. Whereupon the southerners, unable to command or persuade the northern majority, withdrew from the assembly.

Now the last remaining national party, the Democrats, broke in two. The last bond holding the sections together was sundered. Civil war was then at hand.

One group of the Charleston conference met again at Baltimore. There they nominated Stephen A. Douglas of Illinois. He was ready to open the territories to slavery but he was not ready to offer the planters unconditional supremacy in the Democratic party or the Union.

Another group of Democrats chose as their candidate John C. Breckinridge of Kentucky, an out-and-out advocate of the slaveholding interest.

John Bell became the candidate of the Constitutional Union party. It was composed of Whigs and other conservatives who were for the preservation of the Union.

The Republicans, delighted by the confusion among the Democrats, held their convention at Chicago. It declared for liberty for the territories, free homesteads for farmers, a protective tariff, and a Pacific railroad.

The convention nominated Abraham Lincoln of Illinois. "Whatever party name he might call himself by," notes Parrington, "in his love of justice and his warm humanity Lincoln was essentially Jeffersonian. . . ." Business men trusted this man who had been a railroad lawyer. On the tariff, Bank, currency, and homestead issues, he was "sound." He disliked slavery, but he was no abolitionist, and had once said that he saw no way in which the institution could be uprooted. Yet he had also told the country that a house divided against itself could not stand, while he had also said something with which no southern planter would disagree: namely, that the country would become all slave or all free. Lincoln, moreover, disagreed with Seward's concept that there was a "higher law" than the Constitution, dedicating the territories to freedom. But he believed quite positively that slavery should not be permitted in the territories.

The Democratic party had two sets of candidates. The one headed by Douglas was the choice of the North. The other, headed by Breckinridge, was the choice of the South. This division would ensure Lincoln's election.

During the campaign, Republicans resorted to parades and demonstrations

LIBRARY OF CONGRESS COLLECTIONS

The Democrats split and Lincoln becomes President

such as had been used in the log-cabin crusade for General Harrison. But Lincoln remained at home in Springfield and said nothing. His advisers were aware that, as a Republican newspaper put it, "Frémont had tried running on the slavery issue and lost."

The Republican campaign was carried to the country, however, by such able men as Carl Schurz, W. H. Seward, and Horace Greeley, who appealed to the diverse interests of diverse groups. Douglas spoke to throngs in nearly every state of the Union, while Breckinridge men, so convinced were they of the soundness of their position, spoke even in the North.

When the votes were counted it was found that those opposed to slavery agitation had carried the country by an overwhelming majority. Their combined vote was a million more than Lincoln's total. The two Democratic factions alone, to say nothing of the six hundred thousand who voted for Bell, outnumbered the Republican voters. But Lincoln had won the Presidency. It did not matter that he was the choice of a minority—even of a sectional minority. Under the Constitution, he was President of the United States.

The Democratic party emerged from the campaign of 1860 with huge losses. It was not only that it had lost strength in the North. It was also that its stronghold, the South, had left the Union.

For sixty years the Party had had almost unbroken control of the government; sixty dynamic years in the history of the young, turbulent republic. But thereafter, for a long time, it would be a minority party, sometimes strong, sometimes weak.

14

At his inaugural on March 4, 1861, the new President warned the South in these words:

"In your hands, my dissatisfied fellow countrymen, and not in mine, is the momentous issue of civil war. The government will not assail you. You can have no conflict without being yourselves the aggressors. You have no oath registered in heaven to destroy the government, while I shall have the most solemn one to 'preserve, protect, and defend' it."

Then he pleaded with the South in these words:

"We are not enemies, but friends. We must not be enemies. Though passion may have strained, it must not break, our bonds of affection. The mystic chords of memory, stretching from every battlefield and patriot grave to every living heart and hearthstone all over this broad land, will yet swell the chorus of the Union when again touched, as surely they will be, by the better angels of our nature."

This was not to be. A month later Confederate batteries opened fire on Fort Sumter in Charleston harbor.

As the Civil War went its bloody way, many Republicans felt that the President ought not be renominated because he could not be elected while victory after victory on the battlefield was going to the Confederates. The regular Republican nominating convention, however, nominated him by almost unanimous vote on the first ballot, with Andrew Johnson, a Democrat from the border state of Tennessee, as his running mate.

After the convention, when a delegation from the National Union League called on Lincoln to congratulate him, the President used a phrase that has since become part of the American language while sometimes its substance has become the basis of a political campaign:

"I do not allow myself," said the President, "to suppose that either the convention or the League have concluded to decide that I am either the greatest or best man in America, but rather that they have concluded it is best not to swap horses while crossing the river. . . ."

The election of 1864 posed a peculiar problem to Democrats since it came in the midst of the Civil War. Solidly Democratic states had left the Union. Yet the Democratic case did not seem hopeless because the war had dragged on so long and masses of people yearned for peace. Lincoln's cabinet was torn with discord, and many ex-Whigs were displeased with the Emancipation Proclamation. If the war should continue to drag on, it was the belief of many, including Lincoln, that the Republicans might be beaten in the election.

LIBRARY OF CONGRESS COLLECTIONS

The starting point of the great War Between the States—inauguration of Jefferson Davis

LIBRARY OF CONGRESS COLLECTIONS

Philippi, West Virginia, scene of the first battle of the Rebellion, fought June 3, 1861

Ruins of Gallego flour mills, Richmond, Virginia

LIBRARY OF CONGRESS COLLECTIONS

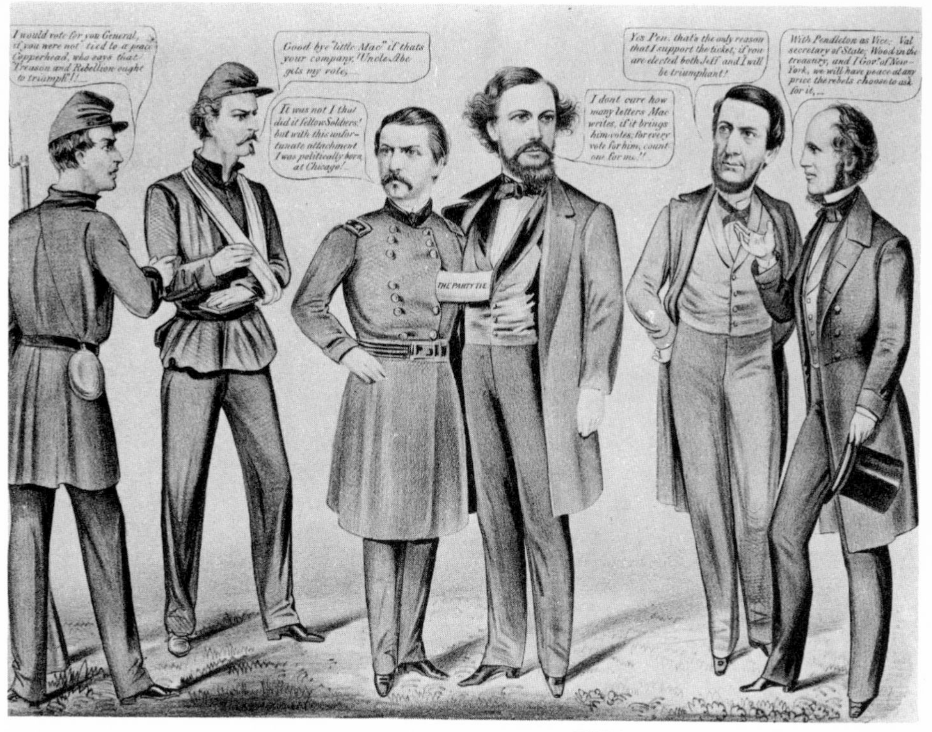

LIBRARY OF CONGRESS COLLECTIONS

Lincoln's ex-General McClellan runs against him as a Democrat in 1865

The Democrats nominated General McClellan as their candidate for the Presidency. Their platform ranged from the weak to the ridiculous. It was weak because it said nothing about the important issues of the tariff and the banking system. It was absurd because it charged the Republicans with doing everything wrong—which was not true—and because, in incomprehensible language, it seemed to demand that the war ought to be stopped. If the Union had stopped the war, the South would have regarded herself as victorious and the world would have recognized her as an independent nation.

It was a grievous lapse that the Democrats did not protest the raising of tariffs, the giving away of thirty million acres of public lands to western railroads, and the setting up of a national banking system in 1863 and 1864. This meant the undoing of the greatest victory of the Jackson era, and the creation of a centralized money factory, beloved of Hamiltonians and Whigs. The Republican banking system then established lasted until 1913, a period of fifty years. Its effects upon the country were stated by Professor J. G. Randall:

"Though it had some merit," he said, "it created an inelastic currency, tended toward the concentration of bank resources in New York, [and] opened the way for serious abuse in the speculative exploitation of bank funds."

LIBRARY OF CONGRESS COLLECTIONS

The Union must and shall be preserved

Democrats, however, did not exhaust their capacity for poor leadership and intellectual laziness in the platform of 1864. They would demonstrate through many platforms in years to come that they were second to none in their ability to sustain a continuing mood of poor leadership and intellectual laziness.

General McClellan ignored the anti-war plank of his party's platform and confused things the more by saying that "No peace can be permanent without Union." He asked men's votes on the implication perhaps that if he were President the war would continue until the Union was saved. Yet, although Democrats and their candidate had achieved a masterwork of confusion, Republican leaders were fearful of losing the election. Horace Greeley said, "Mr. Lincoln cannot be elected," while the editor of the *New York Times* told the President that his chances in the election were dim.

But the tide turned. It turned on bayonets. Farragut became master of Mobile Bay. Sherman took Atlanta. The Union, at long last, was winning. Lincoln received 2,213,600 popular votes; McClellan 1,802,000 votes.

At Lincoln's second inaugural, the war was nearing its end. Then he spoke the words ever green:

"With malice toward none, with charity for all, with firmness in the right as God gives us to see the right, let us strive on to finish the work we are in, to bind up the nation's wounds, to care for him who shall have borne the battle and for his widow and his orphan, to all which may achieve and cherish a just and lasting peace among ourselves and with all nations."

As spring came flooding up the valley of Virginia, Lee surrendered at Appomattox. Six days later, on the morning of April 15, 1865, Lincoln died. A few hours thereafter Andrew Johnson became President of the United States.

15

It soon became apparent that the greedy and the powerful were having their way. Moving under the pretext of war necessity, even before the war was over, Republicans got the tariff they wanted, the national banking system they wanted, and the centralized government they desired. Events proved the accuracy of southern leaders who had predicted that the South would be exploited if the Hamiltonian system should prevail, but they could not anticipate that Republicans would push the system far beyond anything that Hamilton ever contemplated.

The Republican party—especially in the Northeast—had supplanted the Whigs as political agents of the banking, railroad, and industrial interests. "Before 1861," writes Arthur S. Link in *American Epoch*, "a tenuous alliance of the South and West in the Democratic party had held the non-agrarian interests in check and had prevented them from using the federal government to underwrite their program. The withdrawal of the Southern delegations from Congress in 1860–1861, however, threw political control into the hands of the Republican agents of the business classes."

By the end of the war the stage was set for a devastating imperialism. Charles Sumner, indefatigable leader in the process of destruction, said: "The whole broad Rebel region is *tabula rasa,* or clean slate . . . where Congress may write the laws." The West was also a clean slate. It was undeveloped, much of it was territory (not states) and could therefore be controlled by Congress.

The South and the West were the richest parts of the nation in terms of natural resources. They would have become the nation's richest regions if they had been developed, not for the benefit of exploiters of the Northeast, but for the people of the regions and the nation.

Radical Republicans who feared that Lincoln's "tenderhearted" policies toward the South would be executed, took cheer when Johnson succeeded to the Presidency. They believed they could control him. Johnson, however, planned to bring the Confederate states quickly back into the Union without changing the agrarian control they had once held. But when Republican leaders realized that Johnson's plan might restore control of Congress to the agrarian West and South, and that the President meant to be as generous to the defeated South as Lincoln might have been, they moved to overthrow Johnsonian reconstruction and enact their own program.

In the process, Republican leaders impeached the President, and after a trial that kept the country in a state of feverish excitement, he was acquitted by the margin of one vote. This single vote saved the presidential office, as created by the Constitution, from destruction.

The Civil War was an economic revolution and no understanding of the Democratic party is possible unless it is understood that this is the key to Democratic party history for most of the period since 1865. Since that time the Republican party has sought to defend, and whenever possible expand, the economic revolution that came with the war. And the Democratic party, whenever it has not relapsed into semi-coma, has sought to undo that revolution.

The stakes of the battle were so high in 1865 that the Republican party, in order to stay in power, was willing to alienate the white South, impeach the President, muzzle the Supreme Court, and suspend the Constitution. The men who did this were practical men. They were not concerned with a theory, with Negro welfare, or even jobs. They were concerned with the economic program that the Republican party had rammed through during the war and postwar years.

But suppose the Southern Democrats should return to Congress? Then the program might be lost and with it all the immeasurable riches that would accrue to those who were free to plunder an actually rich, and potentially richer, continent. If the Democrats controlled Congress this would mean the repeal of high tariffs whose beneficiaries reaped millions. It would mean the end of colossal land grants to railroads. The new national banking system would be modified and an inflation policy adopted through the issuance of greenbacks and the payment of bonds in this legal tender.

"It is this consideration," writes Professor Henry Commager, "which explains the significance of the election of 1866, the necessity of the guarantees of the Fourteenth Amendment, and the desire for Republican votes in the South embodied in the Fifteenth Amendment."

Four days after the acquittal of Johnson of the impeachment charges, the Republican nominating convention met in Chicago.

It nominated for the Presidency General Ulysses S. Grant, the only candidate whose name was mentioned. The fall elections of 1867 had shown marked Democratic strength, and Republicans wanted a sure-fire candidate. Grant seemed to have the necessary qualifications.

He was a popular war hero. He did not talk much. He had a clean record. He was folksy. He was bereft of all ideas, including political ideas. Indeed no one seemed to know whether he was a Republican or a Democrat, but because he had voted Democratic in the presidential election of 1856, it might have been thought that he would align himself with the Democrats.

The Democratic party was never weaker than in the years following Appomattox. It had no leaders. Only one northern state had a Democratic governor. When Congress met in December 1865, there were only ten Democratic senators out of fifty-two, and only forty Democratic representatives out of a hundred and eighty-five. They did oppose many of the Reconstruction acts, but in general Democratic officeholders seemed to lack both a program and principles.

LIBRARY OF CONGRESS COLLECTIONS

The Democrats looked down their noses, but Grant won

In 1868, at a New York city convention, the Democrats nominated as their candidate for the Presidency, Governor Horatio Seymour of New York, a "dark horse."

The Republicans amassed a large war chest and, wrote the historian Oberholtzer, "At no time before in the history of presidential elections . . . was a candidate put under so great a burden of obligation to rich men, which he would be asked to repay."

The amazing fact of the election is that Grant won by only 300,000 popular votes out of a total of 5,750,000, and since few white Southern Democrats were permitted to vote, he did not receive a majority of the white vote of the nation. But the southern Negro vote gave him a popular majority and he received an overwhelming majority in the electoral college.

It is the melancholy distinction of Grant that he proved to be the most harmful President the country ever had.

16

Now was come the Age of the Spoilsmen. It proceeded upon the principle enunciated by one of the principal spoilsmen, Jim Fisk: "Nothing is lost save honor." From 1865 to the end of the nineteenth century the United States grew mightily as it imported millions of immigrants, built railroads, and exploited its huge resources of oil, forests, land, metals, coal. No other period of the nation's history exhibits such a domination of its life by the industrialist.

In business and politics the "captains of industry," as Thomas Carlyle had dubbed their English counterparts, worked boldly and cynically to achieve their ends. They exploited workers. They milked farmers. They bought legislatures. They spied upon competitors. They hired armed guards. They dynamited property. They used force and intrigue.

When Collis P. Huntington, lord of the Southern Pacific Railroad, wrote to a political agent concerning a bribery for his company, he was expressing the sentiments of most of his industrialist contemporaries:

"If you have to pay money to have the right thing done, it is only just and fair to do it . . . If a man has the power to do great evil and won't do right unless he is bribed to do it, I think the time spent will be gained when it is a man's duty to go up and bribe the judge. A man that will cry out against them himself will also do these things himself. If there was none for it, I would not hesitate."

As businessmen were corrupt, so were hordes of politicians. Such was the practice of thievery. Lord Bryce, author of *The American Commonwealth*, found that the cohesive force in American politics was "the desire for office and for office *as a means of gain.*"

There was then little to distinguish one great political party from the other, and in 1879 the young Woodrow Wilson spoke with disgust of American politics: "No leaders, no principles; no principles, no parties."

The Republicans, however, were successful and, says Hofstadter in *The American Political Tradition,* "From . . . Reconstruction onwards . . . the Republican Party existed in an unholy conjunction with the capitalistic interests. . . . Before business learned to buy statesmen at wholesale, it had to buy privileges at retail. Fabulous sums were spent. A disgruntled Congressman from Ohio declared in 1873 that 'the House of Representatives was like an auction room where more valuable considerations were disposed of under the hammer than in any other place on earth.' Between 1866 and 1872 . . . the Union Pacific spent $400,000 on bribes. Little wonder that an honest Republican . . . like Walter Q. Gresham could describe his party as 'an infernally corrupt concern,' or that Senator Grimes of Iowa, once an important leader, could say in 1870: 'I believe it is today the most corrupt and debauched political party that ever existed. . . .' "

This was the noisome political atmosphere of the nation when Grant took office, during his administrations, and long afterward.

Under Grant, the government was less a government than a business. More and more men enriched themselves through corruption. The pickings were lush. In the twenty-five-year period that ended in 1872, the Government gave to the railroads lands equal in area to Maine, New Hampshire, Vermont, Massachusetts, Rhode Island, Connecticut, and a large part of Pennsylvania. The Union Pacific got huge tracts of land on both sides of track, and an enormous loan secured by a second mortgage. Land grabbers worked on an imperial scale. "A chart of the railway land grants in the West," wrote the Beards, "looms up like the map of the Roman Empire in the age of Augustus."

Grant enormously admired the great capitalists. He believed with Carnegie and Rockefeller that God had intended to turn over to these worthies the control of just as much of the world as they could grasp. The worthies, for their part, grabbed everything in sight, and through graft and fraudulent practices reduced the morality of the government to the lowest estate it has ever known.

Yet, because there was "prosperity" in the land, there was little protest from the people that their country was being debauched. Henry Adams concluded that the public did not care about reform: "The moral law had expired—like the Constitution." Since the public attitude toward political corruption then—and now—was often compounded of equal parts of self-righteousness, smugness, and apathy, it may be well to note what Horatio Seymour said on this subject in a letter to Tilden: "Our people want men in office who will not steal, but who will not interfere with those who do."

Republicans again nominated Grant in 1872 and again raised a great war chest. They relied more upon the concussions of cash than the cogencies of reason.

Liberal Republicans, rebelling against the corruptions of Grant's first term, nominated Horace Greeley for the Presidency. Their platform denounced the Grant Administration, and demanded an end to the horrors of Reconstruction and removal of all disabilities from the southern people.

The Democrats, who had no alternative to Grant, no ideas, and almost no sense, had no candidate or platform of their own. They adopted the candidate and platform of the liberal Republicans. It did not seem to matter to them that since Greeley had been an abusive enemy of the Democrats, and since they were supporting him simply because they felt he might beat Grant, they were clearly demonstrating their moral and intellectual bankruptcy.

The so-called Straight Democrats—those who refused to support Greeley—nominated Charles O'Conor for the Presidency.

"It was one of the strangest campaigns in history," wrote Professor J. G. Randall. "Republicans excoriated a Republican President; Liberals labored without enthusiasm for a candidate whose choice was intolerable to them; Democrats supported a violent and abusive opponent; ex-Confederates . . . did battle for a foe who had denounced them as traitors and rebels."

The electorate, concluding perhaps that if Grant was bad, the other candidates were worse, chose Grant again.

17

Corruption is a poisonous plant that becomes well rooted only after the passage of a little time. As Grant's second administration got under way, it flowered widely.

Item: The Navy Department sold business to contractors.

Item: The Department of the Interior enriched land speculators and got a few pennies for itself in the dealings.

Item: The "whiskey ring," composed of revenue officers and distillers, defrauded Uncle Sam of millions.

Item: The United States Minister to Brazil, remote from the looting at home and growing restive because of his inability to steal anything, defrauded the Brazilian Government of $100,000. He then ran away and left it up to Washington to pay the bill.

A merry time was had by all as scandal followed scandal, grafters and thieves manipulated the wooden-Indian President (he was personally honest), and public morality sank lower and lower.

But it was not the corruption of the Grant Administration that moved the people to effective protest against it. The Panic of 1873 became a depression that brought bankruptcy and unemployment on a wide scale. It was the Depression

—and not all the mountainous accumulation of fraud and corruption—that brought crushing defeat to the Republicans in the mid-term election of 1874. For the first time since 1865 Democrats were in control of the lower house, while the Republican majority in the Senate was greatly reduced.

Democratic prospects looked better. Southern whites were again coming into power despite Reconstruction, and their votes hereafter would count. Furthermore, Republicans were now as lacking in leadership as the Democrats—a feat of some proportions.

Grant had third-term dreams, but in the election of 1876 Republicans nominated the "dark horse" Rutherford B. Hayes of Ohio.

Their platform castigated "sin." It was agin' polygamy. This was safe. What one might call the polygamous-minded among us—yesterday or today—have never espoused plural polygamy (the illegal variety) but serial polygamy—one girl after another. This is not illegal but is merely offensive to one's wife, neighbors, children, and perhaps the husbands of the "girls."

The platform was also for tariff protection. It said that public officers should be held to rigid responsibility, but it seems never to have heard of the goings-on of the Grant Administration.

The Democrats chose Samuel J. Tilden, Governor of New York, as their presidential candidate. Prosecutor of the Tweed Ring—a colossal, localized Democratic contribution to corruption—he was opposed by the worthies of Tammany Hall.

It is part of the license of American political campaigns that one party may make charges against the other that are wide of the mark. But the Democratic platform of 1876 commented accurately on the record of the Grant Administration:

> When the annals of this Republic show the disgrace and censure of a Vice-President; a late Speaker of the House of Representatives marketing his rulings as a presiding officer; three senators profiting secretly by their votes as law makers; five chairmen of the leading committees of the House of Representatives exposed in jobbery; a late Secretary of the Treasury forcing balances in the public accounts; a late Attorney General misappropriating public funds; a Secretary of the Navy enriched or enriching friends by percentages levied off the profits of contractors with his department; an Ambassador to England censured in a dishonorable speculation; the President's private secretary barely escaping conviction upon trial for guilty complicity in frauds upon the revenue; a Secretary of War impeached for high crimes and misdemeanors—the demonstration is complete that the first step in reform must be the people's choice of honest men from another party.

By midnight of election day, Tilden supporters were sure that their man had been elected President, and Hayes went to bed believing that he had lost the election. Tilden had received nearly 250,000 more popular votes than Hayes. In the electoral college, where 185 votes were necessary for election, he had 184

The bitterly contested Hayes-Tilden election

NEW YORK PUBLIC LIBRARY

LIBRARY OF CONGRESS COLLECTIONS

Then, as now, a state secret was a rumor heard in retrospect undisputed votes. Hayes had 165 undisputed votes, and 20 votes were contested. Nineteen of these votes were from the South, where chaos still reigned under Reconstruction. A commission, containing a majority of Republicans, gave all the doubtful votes to Hayes and he was declared elected.

The phrase "Tilden or blood" was on many Democratic lips and it is likely that the South would not have accepted Hayes without bloodshed if the Republicans, as the price of keeping Hayes in peace, had not promised to withdraw federal troops from Louisiana and South Carolina, the last two carpetbag states. The promise was kept and Reconstruction drew to an end.

Who was in the right in the contested election? It would appear, as one historian has suggested, that the Democrats stole the election in South Carolina, Florida and Louisiana—the states from which nineteen disputed electors were returned. Then the Republicans stole back the stolen election. And if men never succeed in getting nearer to the truth of the election than this, it is all reminiscent of the title of Fielding's play—*Rape upon Rape, or, Justice Caught in His Own Trap*.

Radical Reconstruction, a dark interlude in southern history, ended in the Hayes Administration in 1877. By that time, however, the reconstruction of national politics that began with the outbreak of the war in 1861 had achieved its goals. The business classes had executed a bloodless revolution. Outwardly all seemed the same since the structure of American political institutions had not been altered. But the business groups had wrested control of political institutions from the agrarian majority. Then they proceeded to change the character, but not the forms, of American representative government.

Although Democratic cartoons pictured Hayes with "fraud" over his brow, his enemies called him "Rutherfraud," and people were mindful of the manner in which he became President, he nonetheless gave the country an honest administration.

Democratic spirits had fallen low as the White House, that had seemed so near, was suddenly snatched from them; but their hopes rose in 1878 when they won control of both houses of Congress. In 1879 their hopes fell. It was an immensely prosperous year, crops failed in Europe, and the Indian cotton crop was short. All this gave promise of continued exports, continued prosperity, continued Republican rule.

Republicans chose James A. Garfield as their candidate in the election of 1880, with Chester A. Arthur as Vice-Presidential candidate.

The Democrats picked as their candidate a nonentity named General Winfield S. Hancock. Their platform—a kind of high wind in Jamaica document—pictured the Democratic party as purer than probationer angels, and said Republicans were guilty of what evangelists called "sins incarnadine." The Republicans again concentrated their efforts against polygamy.

This was a period of complete political bankruptcy. "Neither Democrats nor Republicans," wrote John D. Hicks, "seemed to sense the significance of the vast transformation that was coming over business, nor the critical nature of the relationship between labor and capital . . . The Republican Party existed to oppose the Democratic Party. Real issues cut across both parties, and even when recognized . . . had to be evaded or ignored. . . ."

Garfield, sanctimonious and tainted by only a few major scandals, essentially a decent man, was elected. Four months after his inauguration he was shot by a disgruntled office-seeker and was succeeded by the Vice-President, Chester A. Arthur, who had only recently been a spoilsman's spoilsman as a member of Roscoe Conkling's New York Customhouse machine.

18

During the Garfield and Arthur régimes there emerged on the national scene a man who would dominate the Democratic party from 1884 to 1896, and who in terms of honesty and independence, if nothing else, proved the only man gifted with the qualities of a major president in the long line between Lincoln and Theodore Roosevelt. Grover Cleveland, son of a poor, studious Presbyterian parson, was thrown on his own resources at an early age in his native city of Buffalo, New York. Rugged, fat, amiable, he soon joined what Professor Allan Nevins calls "the hotel lobby and bar-room set."

Unusually honest for the Gilded Age, Cleveland had been sheriff and mayor of Buffalo, and Governor of New York, before he became President. "We have had more brilliant Presidents than Cleveland," wrote H. L. Mencken, "but we have never had one, at least since Washington, whose fundamental character was solider and more admirable . . . He came into office his own man, and he went out without yielding anything of that character . . ."

When the campaign of 1884 approached, Republican leaders were in a dilemma. Arthur was impossible. Grant lay dying. Blaine's public record, after all the defenses and apologies had been made, was distressing for the reformers to behold. But he was nominated nonetheless on the plea that he had "earned the nomination." Yet this man, whom Republicans had twice rejected because of his gamey reputation, could not be washed clean. He aroused the distrust and enmity of those whom Theodore Roosevelt styled "the most virtuous and desirable men of the great seaboard cities."

His nomination stuck in the throats of many Republicans. They had been appalled to witness the party of Lincoln degenerate into the party of Grant, Garfield, and—Blaine. Derisively called "Mugwumps," although calling themselves

Independent Republicans, they supported Cleveland in the election of 1884, because they detested a man who, as the famous editor Godkin said, "had wallowed in spoils like a rhinoceros in an African pool."

The Democratic platform was silly and weak. It was silly because it did little except abuse the opposing party. It was weak because it dodged nearly all the important issues of the day and offered no positive program.

Since the Democrats, then, were running almost entirely on Cleveland's personal honesty, Republicans snooped around and came up with the interesting fact that he had an illegitimate child. This engaged the attention of the country for two reasons. The first is that, among us, no brother need look for a keeper because millions of us long to be our brother's keeper. The second is that, by a curious moral blindness, we tend to associate "immorality" almost exclusively with any sexual expression outside the holy bond of wedlock, the immorality being the greater if one is found out, for then a penalty attaches to it. Thus, when a North Carolina politician, a good church member and family man, was caught by the political opposition where he ought not to have been, with a lady he ought not to have been with, his political career was ended. And when friends consoled him by saying, "Well, Bill, you didn't do anything that all of us haven't done," he replied in terms of our pragmatic morality, "Yes, but by God, you didn't read about it the next morning in the Raleigh *News and Observer.*"

Soon, to return to Cleveland, everybody was gabbing about the little bastard of the Democratic presidential candidate, and Republicans were singing a popular ditty that went:

Ma! Ma! Where's my pa?
Gone to the White House.
Ha! Ha! Ha!

Few were now concerned with national problems that really concerned them, problems having to do with labor, agriculture, tariffs, and the plutocracy.

Crestfallen Democrats asked Cleveland how he expected to combat the accusations. His answer was "Tell the truth." He admitted freely that he had "sinned" with Maria Halpin. But he did not know whether the child was his. And neither, it appeared, did the tippling Mrs. Halpin.

Democrats argued, in effect, that the issue was not what a candidate had done in bed, but what he might do in office. "We are told that Mr. Blaine has been delinquent in office but blameless in private life," a Mugwump said, "while Mr. Cleveland has been a model of official integrity but culpable in his personal relations. We should therefore elect Mr. Cleveland to the public office which he is so well qualified to fill and remand Mr. Blaine to the private station which he is admirably fitted to adorn."

Excess tends to breed excess. Hence there was little shyness when Democrats discussed Blaine's dishonesty. But Tammany opposed Cleveland and he was saved perhaps only by the absurd incident of Dr. Burchard. He was one of a group of windy clergymen who visited Blaine in New York. There he said to the tired and probably bored man: "We are Republicans and we don't propose to leave our party and identify ourselves with the party whose antecedents are Rum, Romanism, and Rebellion."

That did it, although Blaine had not associated himself with the sentiments of the clergyman. Democrats quickly circulated Dr. Burchard's foot-in-mouth remarks throughout eastern cities, and especially New York where the Irish Catholic vote was of decisive importance. Blaine lost New York by only 1,140 votes out of more than a million. It is probable that if the clergyman had kept his sentiments to himself, alliteration and all, Blaine would have become President.

LIBRARY OF CONGRESS COLLECTIONS

First Democratic president since before the war—Grover Cleveland

Mrs. Grover Cleveland—one of the most beautiful of First Ladies

LIBRARY OF CONGRESS COLLECTIONS

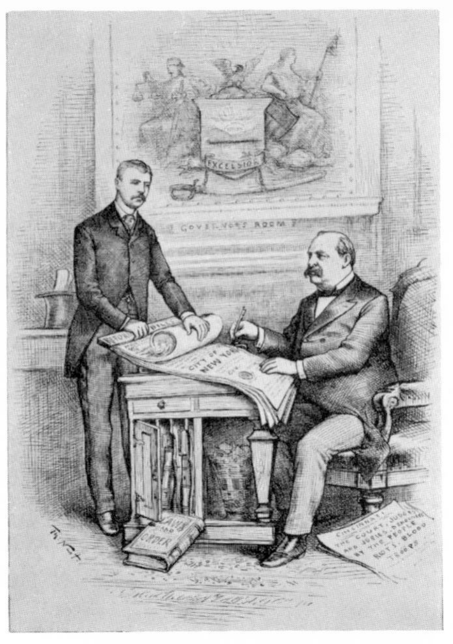

LIBRARY OF CONGRESS COLLECTIONS

Reform without bloodshed—
Governor Cleveland and Theodore Roosevelt
at their good work

LIBRARY OF CONGRESS COLLECTIONS

The Democratic Convention
at Chicago, 1884—some characteristic
features of the city

Spellbinding in German—
a meeting of Germans for Cleveland
in the New York Academy of Music

LIBRARY OF CONGRESS COLLECTIONS

As Brooklyn goes . . .

LIBRARY OF CONGRESS COLLECTIONS

LIBRARY OF CONGRESS COLLECTIONS

Wishful thinking by Democrats

LIBRARY OF CONGRESS COLLECTIONS

The election returns—the extraordinary spectacle in Printing-house Square on the night of November 1, 1884

One of the first fruits of the victory. President-elect Cleveland: "Shake heartily, boys!"

LIBRARY OF CONGRESS COLLECTIONS

Unaccustomed though they were, Democrats now occupied the White House after a lapse of twenty-four years. And much to the chagrin of the Republicans, a Democrat-administered country survived and flourished. But although the new President exhibited strength and even nobility, he had no constructive program to present to the nation. He did, however, satisfy the appetites of hungry Democrats by removing four-fifths of the fourth-class postmasters, all the internal revenue agents, and ten-elevenths of the collectors. A Republican army gave way to an army of "deserving" Democrats, but Mugwumps were displeased because they believed Cleveland had become the captive of party bosses. The new President was a handy man with a veto. Among others, he vetoed more than two hundred pension bills for veterans of the Grand Army of the Republic, and disappointed Republicans yearning for the pension trough. He vetoed a rivers and harbors bill —always the hunting ground of the politically faithful—and snatched manna from the mouths of contractors whom the government had long fed as the Lord had fed Elijah in the desert. He also wrested from corporations and individuals more than eighty million acres of land stolen from Uncle Sam during régimes of his predecessors.

Perhaps men could have stood all this, if Cleveland had not assailed the holy of holies by attacking the moral principles of the protective tariff. Rates were then just about what they had been in 1866 and Democrats, for all their piety in the matter, had made no frontal attack on the tariff as Calhoun had done. But

An independent victory. The Democratic party was compelled to nominate a man with a clean record—one whose knees will not yield, even to Boss Kelly.

LIBRARY OF CONGRESS COLLECTIONS

LIBRARY OF CONGRESS COLLECTIONS

The Panic—scenes in Wall Street Wednesday morning, May 14, 1884

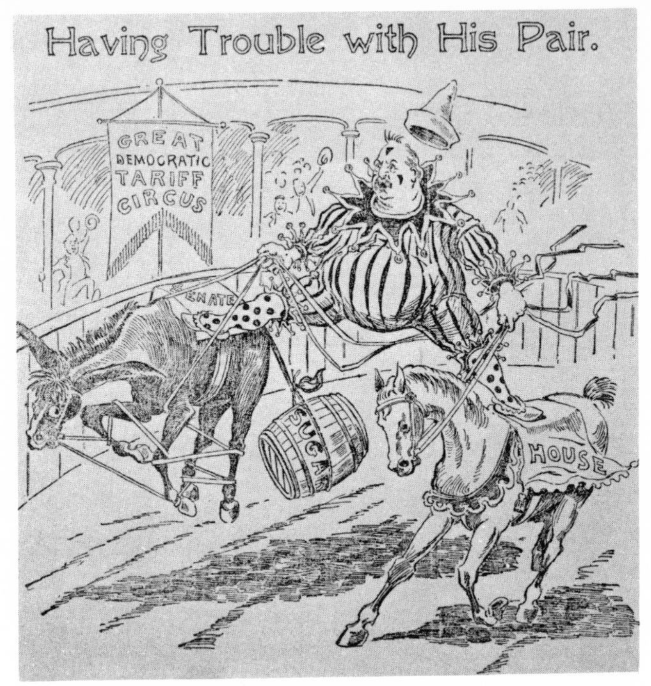

LIBRARY OF CONGRESS COLLECTIONS

IF NOT CLEVELAND, *WHO?*

Prompt and Potential Replies to The World's Important Question Yesterday.

LOGICAL DEMOCRATIC CANDIDATE.

West and South Aroused from Political Lethargy by the Mere Suggestion.

SOME HOT SHOTS AT MR. CLEVELAND.

Leaders in the Party Organization Declare He Could Not Carry Half the Southern States.

NEW ENGLAND AND NEW YORK APPROVE.

LIBRARY OF CONGRESS COLLECTIONS

Cleveland becomes a candidate again in 1892

Cleveland said that the protective tariff was vicious and inequitable, and taxed every American "for the benefit of the manufacturers."

Industrial barons thereupon screamed as though they were being subjected to kidney surgery without benefit of chloroform, and started beating the bushes for a man who could lick Cleveland in the next election. Their choice was Benjamin Harrison, grandson of the ninth President, and a Blaine supporter.

19

In the election of 1888 the tariff was the only issue. Republicans who had waxed fat under tariff protection ladled out money for the campaign, and Boss Matt Quay told campaign managers: "Put the manufacturers of Pennsylvania under the fire and dry all the fat out of them." The fires burned, the fat dripped, and three million dollars—a huge sum for the time—went into the campaign chest.

Cleveland received a majority of the popular votes, but Harrison became President through bribery, intrigue, and fraud practiced in his behalf but without his connivance. He was an innocent, unworldly man and when he heard the election results, he said happily: "Providence has given us the victory." This display of naïveté irritated the hard-bitten Matt Quay. He knew that money, more than the Lord, had turned the tide in Indiana and elsewhere. "Think of the man," he snorted. "He ought to know that Providence hadn't a damn thing to do with it." He added that Harrison would never know "how close a number of men were compelled to approach the gates of the penitentiary to make him President."

Weak, naïve, bewildered, Harrison did as he was told by party bosses, and was an unwitting tool of privilege-grabbers. Under him, Congress passed the McKinley tariff bill. It increased duties on manufactures and put added millions into industrialists' pockets.

Cleveland had left a large surplus in the Treasury. But it soon disappeared as pension bills and rivers and harbors bills came through—so fast that within two years the government needed money.

But in the mid-term congressional election the Republican majority was swept out of the House of Representatives. Southern and western farmers, bitter against railroads, bankers, monopolies, and big business control of government, organized a third party. One of its leaders, Mary Lease, told them to "raise less corn and more hell."

This party—the Populists—nominated James B. Weaver for the Presidency, the Republicans renominated Harrison, and the Democrats chose Grover Cleveland with Adlai E. Stevenson, of Illinois, for Vice-President.

Cleveland was decisively elected but he had hardly begun his second term when the Panic of 1893 swept the country.

LIBRARY OF CONGRESS COLLECTIONS

The campaign of '92—Grover Cleveland of New York for President, Adlai E. Stevenson of Illinois for Vice-President

Miss Democracy—"Now, dear, give me a sweet kiss and you shall have this stick of candy"

LIBRARY OF CONGRESS COLLECTIONS

LIBRARY OF CONGRESS COLLECTIONS

Again the country faced the silver question and economic sectionalism. It is too complicated to be examined here in detail, but this may be said of it: Ever since 1865 southern and western farmers had annually created great wealth in the form of cotton and wheat crops. But for thirty years they had watched prices of their products go down while everything they bought went up, until the dollar had almost trebled in value. The debt that a man could once have paid with 1,000 bushels of wheat now cost him 3,000. The farmer concluded that his troubles arose from the scarcity of money, and that they would cease if there should be an increase of the money supply. Debtors wanted cheap and plentiful money. Creditors wanted high and scarce money. This was the crux of the silver quarrel.

There began a fierce agrarian revolt. The rebels swept state legislatures, reached Congress, and frightened business by their vehemence. Farmers were being converted to "progressivism." They were ready to abandon laissez faire for a program of governmental intervention in economic affairs. Neither of the great political parties could ignore this movement.

The economic situation of the country deteriorated and the year 1894 was the worst that Americans had known for thirty years. Prices and wages seemed to find no bottom. Over half a million workers went on strike against intolerable conditions, but most of the strikes failed. Ragged and hungry bands of men swarmed over the countryside, and popular discontent rose to fever pitch as everything seemed to conspire to convince the people that democracy was a failure.

Here let us pause for a brief backward look. From the earliest days of the government until 1833, the Democratic Party had inhibited the growth of the Hamiltonian system. From 1833 to 1861 the Party had kept it in abeyance. But from 1861 onward the system overshadowed the nation. Now farmers were being victimized by railroads, middlemen, tariffs, speculators, warehousemen, and monopolistic manufacturers of farm equipment.

Cleveland asked for repeal of the Silver Purchase Act. He believed that the gold standard was a standard of honor and bimetallism would wreck the nation. Most men then put their faith in the gold standard as in God, and it was therefore heretical to plump for free silver. (This, however, was a continuing belief. In 1933, says Richard Hofstadter, "When Franklin D. Roosevelt took the United States off the gold standard, Lewis W. Douglas was heard to moan: 'Well, this is the end of Western civilization.' ")

Repeal of the Silver Purchase Act would further contract the currency and lower farm prices, and William Jennings Bryan, a member of the House of Representatives, said the gold standard would bring woe to millions of men, "work-worn and dust-begrimed" who "gave to the Democratic Party a name and for whom it has presumed to speak." A sharp party split was in the making when he called gold standard men "imperious, arrogant, compassionateless."

At their nominating convention in Chicago, western and southern agrarians dominated the proceedings and read Cleveland and his followers out of the party. Their new spokesman and leader was William Jennings Bryan, the ex-congressman and editor from Omaha, powerfully built and with some suggestion of a fanatic about him.

At political conventions of both parties there are always orators who "make the welkin ring," or "utter a clarion call." But the silver-tongued orators of 1896 outdid themselves as they praised free silver. In their orations they managed to allude to the following somewhat diverse group of persons and places:

Washington, Jefferson, Madison, Monroe, Jackson, Lincoln, Cincinnatus, Tiberius Gracchus, Cato, Cicero, Catiline, Leonidas, Ivanhoe, Henry of Navarre, Peter the Hermit, Cromwell, Danton, Murat, Robespierre, Napoleon, Wellington, Lodi, Austerlitz, Waterloo, Yorktown, Thermopylae. Strangely, no one mentioned Moses, Joshua, or Armageddon.

As Bryan rose to speak, the hall was tense. "We do not come as aggressors," he said. "We are fighting in defense of our homes, our families, and posterity. We have petitioned and our petitions have been disregarded... We have begged, and they have mocked when our calamity came. We beg no longer, we entreat no more... We defy them."

Then he asked: "Upon which side will the Democratic Party stand; upon the side of 'idle holders of idle capital' or upon the side of the struggling masses... There are two ideas of Government... There are those who believe that if you will only legislate to make the well-to-do prosperous, their prosperity will leak through on those below. *The Democratic idea, however, has been that if you make the masses prosperous, their prosperity will find its way up through every class which rests upon them.*"

The young William Jennings Bryan—
the greatest orator of his times

LIBRARY OF CONGRESS COLLECTIONS

Amid profound silence came the peroration:

"If they dare to come out in the open field and defend the gold standard as a good thing, we will fight them to the uttermost. Having behind us the producing masses of this country and the world, supported by the commercial interests, the laboring interests and the toilers everywhere, we will answer their demand for a gold standard by saying to them: You shall not press down upon the brow of labor this crown of thorns, you shall not crucify mankind on a cross of gold."

The delegates and crowd of eighteen thousand were stirred to hysteria. On the strength of one oration a young ex-congressman was nominated for the Presidency, and the Democratic President then in the White House was repudiated. Viewed coldly, this seems extraordinarily odd, but the Democrats in 1896 represented a movement of passion and despair, the last great farmers' revolt. Vachel Lindsay, in his "Bryan, Bryan, Bryan, Bryan," wrote:

And all these in their helpless days
By the dour East oppressed,
Mean paternalism,
Making their mistakes for them,
Crucifying half the West,
Till the whole Atlantic coast
Seemed a giant spider's nest.

The Democratic candidate for the Presidency, endorsed also by the Populists, advocated free silver coinage and low tariffs, but he was not a radical of the

LIBRARY OF CONGRESS COLLECTIONS

The speech that won the nomination

William Jennings Bryan of Nebraska for President—Adlai E. Stevenson of Illinois for Vice-President

LIBRARY OF CONGRESS COLLECTIONS

Conservatives of both parties
denounce Bryan Democrats as wreckers

LIBRARY OF CONGRESS COLLECTIONS

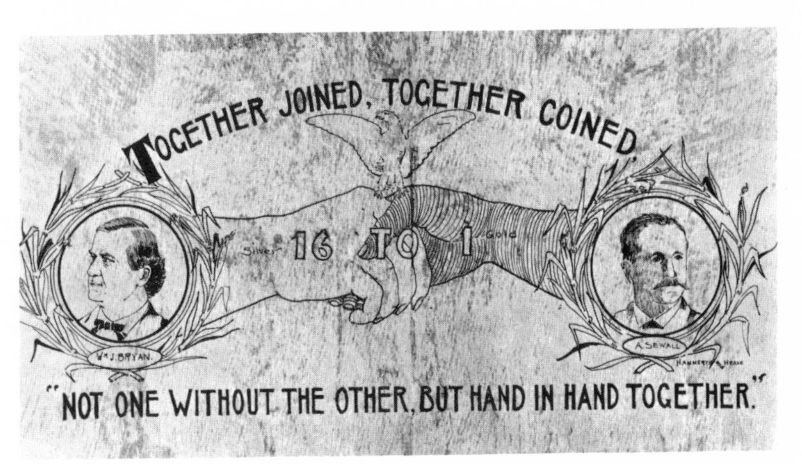

LIBRARY OF CONGRESS COLLECTIONS

Populist variety. Yet the Democratic platform was manna to the Populists since it promised tariff reform, a graduated income tax, prosecution of the trusts. More important, it united the farming West and South in their attempt to capture control of the federal government from the banking-manufacturing East.

Businessmen became alarmed, especially since the Populists had polled more than a million votes four years before and were making gains among the masses of Democrats. Now Marcus A. Hanna, a retired industrialist of great wealth, bored by contemplating his navel, stepped into the lists.

"By a liberal expenditure of money, judicious publicity, and early management of Negro politicians from the South," wrote the Beards, "he made William McKinley the man of the hour."

The presidential election of 1896 was the first in which money was spent on a great scale. Mark Hanna went about it systematically by assessing the business interests that felt themselves threatened by Bryan, and since the silver question endangered the national financial system, headquarters for collecting money were established in New York, the headquarters of national finance.

A torrent of Republican money flowed through the land. Vachel Lindsay described the process as:

> Pouring out the long green to a million workers,
> Spondulix by the mountain-load to stop each new tornado.

Bryan visited twenty-nine states and made some six hundred speeches. But Mark Hanna apparently believed that it was better to let money talk than to let McKinley talk, and kept him silent in Canton, Ohio, throughout the campaign. Intimidation was used as well as money. Businessmen told workers that Bryan's election would mean the loss of their jobs. Orders were placed with manufacturers on the condition that they would be cancelled if Bryan became President, while holders of western mortgages announced that at McKinley's election mortgages would be renewed for five years and interest rates reduced.

McKinley won with about 7,000,000 votes as against 6,500,000 for Bryan.

Republicans, having taken over the government, then took over God. When the votes were counted, Mark Hanna sent a telegram indicative of both his simple faith and his comradely knowledge of God's whereabouts. He said: "God's in His heaven." The New York *Tribune,* with a private wire to heaven, said Bryan had lost "because right is right and God is God."

Bryan had indeed lost but the progressivism he advocated had not lost. It would become a major force in American life and politics. (Many of the programs he espoused became national legislation by the third decade of the twentieth century.) Foreseeing this, Tom Johnson, the distinguished Mayor of Cleveland, Ohio, called the election "the first great protest of the American people against monopoly—the first great struggle of the masses in our country against the privileged classes. It was not free silver that frightened the plutocrat leaders. What they feared then, what they fear now, is free men."

20

As the twentieth century neared, the grip on the government that the nonagrarian interests had achieved at the outset of the Civil War remained as firm as ever. The tariff, the banking system, and the accepted methods of dealing with the public lands had not been shaken by the storms. The philosophy and practice known as Darwinism had not been weakened by doubters. Darwin had seen in the animal world a struggle for survival that destroyed the weak, rewarded the strong, and produced evolutionary change. Advocates of social Darwinism contended that struggle, destruction of the weak, and the survival of the fit were essential to progress in human society. The weak blocked the road to progress and merited destruction. The strong survived because they were superior. This was an elemental law of development. Therefore, the argument concluded, it was futile for government to help the weak to survive.

This obviously ran counter to the humane and Christian principles upon which the American democratic tradition rested. But there could be no mass support of progressivism until religious leaders challenged social Darwinism and joined with the people to make the banking-manufacturing interest responsible to the whole people. By 1900 a humanitarian movement in American Protestantism, called the social gospel, had achieved strength, and soon most of the large denominations were moving toward social Christianity.

Although Bryan had been defeated in 1896 he was firmly established in the leadership of his party. He was again nominated as Democratic candidate for the Presidency in 1900, with Adlai E. Stevenson of Illinois, who was Vice-President during Cleveland's second administration, as his running mate.

A Democratic version of a Horatio Alger hero in 1900

LIBRARY OF CONGRESS COLLECTIONS

The Republicans again chose as their presidential candidate William McKinley. They selected as his running mate Theodore Roosevelt, Spanish War hero and Governor of New York. Mark Hanna thought him "unsafe." But Thomas Platt and Matt Quay, bosses of the New York and Philadelphia machines, forced Hanna to accept him because Platt wanted to get rid of him as Governor of New York. There he was not as pliant as the bosses wanted him to be.

The country was prosperous. It was prosperous, said Republicans, because of high protective tariffs. Nobody really cared what had brought prosperity. The only thing that counted was that nearly everybody was eating high off the hog, and when the votes were counted Bryan had lost by about 850,000 votes and received 21 fewer electoral votes than at his first effort.

Senator Platt, boss of the New York machine, was delighted that he had got rid of the "cowboy" Roosevelt who would now fade away while presiding over the Senate. But on September 6, 1901, McKinley was assassinated, and when he died eight days later the forty-three-year-old Theodore Roosevelt became President.

Before continuing our narrative, let us observe what happened to the Democratic party after Bryan's second defeat. Gold Democrats of the East at once tried to rebuild it but they tried to make the rebuilt party resemble as nearly as possible the party that had existed under Cleveland. They did not really want a Democratic party that had its own mind, its own principles, its own view of men and government. What they wanted was another version of the Republican party that merely went by the name Democratic: respectable, well-tubbed, and even genteel—that shabbiest of all spiritual estates. This party would stand for "Justice," for "Reform," and for a slightly lowered tariff.

But in their quest for gentility, they overlooked one thing no larger than the state of Texas. Who would vote for a party embalmed in gentility?

Theodore Roosevelt lamented that he was President by accident, and had not been elected by the people. But the opportunity to be elected came to him when his party nominated him for the Presidency in 1904, while the Democrats chose Judge Alton B. Parker of New York, with Henry G. Davis of West Virginia in the second place. This was a curious choice. Davis was eighty-one years old. But he was a millionaire and he was given second place on the ticket because it was thought that, out of senility, generosity, or conviction, he would contribute liberally to the campaign fund. The foxy old man fooled them, and Davis wooed did not turn out to be Davis won. He didn't give.

The Democratic campaign of 1904 was, if nothing else, harmonious in all its parts. Since Parker was a meaningless man, the now meaningless Democratic party ran him on a meaningless platform. The candidate and the platform—sedative by day and soporific by night—put most of the voters to sleep. Those who remained awake voted Republican. Roosevelt was elected by a large majority and Congress was strongly Republican.

LIBRARY OF CONGRESS COLLECTIONS

They lost to Theodore Roosevelt and Charles W. Fairbanks in 1904

The lesson had long been plain but, of course, it had not been learned. It is irrational to assume that because men are capable of arriving at rational conclusions, they will necessarily do so. The lesson was this: when the Democratic party is merely a low-church version of the high-church Republican party, and its spiritual anemia makes it as pale as the underbelly of a catfish, it has no appeal for voters and certainly does not deserve their support.

Roosevelt, delighted that he was President by choice of the people, said that "under no circumstances will I be a candidate for or accept another nomination." He would, as the phrase is, live to rue the day he had uttered these words.

Roosevelt did not sympathize with radical rich men or radical labor leaders. In 1906 he wrote: ". . . I have no especial respect or admiration for and trust in the typical big moneyed men of my country. I do not regard them as furnishing sound opinion as regards foreign or domestic policies."

A year later he wrote:

"I neither respect nor admire the huge moneyed men to whom money is the be-all and end-all of existence; to whom the acquisition of untold millions is the supreme goal of life and who are too often utterly indifferent as to how these millions are obtained . . . I despise him, if he does not treat other things as of more importance in his scheme of life than mere money getting; if he does not care for art, or literature, or science, or statecraft, or war craft, or philanthropy."

He condemned Edward H. Harriman, the railroad magnate, as an "undesirable citizen." But he also applied the same epithet to Eugene V. Debs, the labor leader and Socialist candidate for President.

Roosevelt made one important break with the past. He was the first American president who directly proposed to use the powers of the government to accomplish what Huey Long later called "spreading the wealth." In 1906, he avowed his intention "so far as it can be done by legislation, to favor the growth of intelligence and the diffusion of wealth in such a manner as will measurably avoid the extreme of swollen fortunes and grinding poverty . . ." Such a pronouncement was alarming to practical politicians, but Roosevelt, aside from proposing the taxation of "swollen inheritances and incomes," never made it clear how he would accomplish his purpose.

As in the day when it was bad form to mention "social diseases" by their unadorned names, so it was bad form in Roosevelt's day for the President, of all people, not only to suggest that wealth was not distributed with justice and mercy, but that it would be well to restore the balance partially at least through income and inheritance taxes. Even more shocking, here was a President who suggested that since the wisdom of Supreme Court Justices did not descend from on high, they could be just as fallible in their judgments as livery stable owners. He believed that some of them were miles behind the times and had hermetically sealed minds. He said there were "some members of the judicial body who have lagged behind in their understanding of those great and vital changes in the body politic, whose minds have never been opened to the new applications of the old principles made necessary by the new conditions."

Some thirty years later, when Franklin D. Roosevelt struck a similar note, it was not only felt that he had uttered a heresy that would make burning at the stake too good for him, but that it was wholly and peculiarly a *Democratic* heresy.

21

As for the Democratic party, its conservative eastern leaders were now discredited, and no young men of promise or performance were rising to take their place. Bryan's prestige was greater than ever following the disastrous Parker defeat, he still had a huge personal following, his ideas and feelings were in the great tradition of the Democratic party, and in 1908 he became again its undisputed leader.

Here is a record unparalleled in American politics. It is usually enough to destroy a man as a leader if, as the party's presidential candidate, he is once beaten. Bryan, however, who was beaten twice and then surrendered the leadership, came back four years later stronger than ever. The reason is simple. He stood for certain important values. Anti-Bryan Democrats stood for nothing at all.

Republicans chose as their presidential candidate William H. Taft, whom Roosevelt had picked to succeed him in the White House.

Taft won in an unexciting campaign. Bryan had lost for the third time as a presidential candidate, but since the western progressive wing of the Democratic party did better in the election than the conservative eastern wing that aped the Republican party, Bryan four years later would be strongly in position to affect political history at the Baltimore convention by defeating the easterners and forcing the nomination of Woodrow Wilson.

Taft settled down his ponderous 330-pound bulk, along with which went the ripplingest smile and the most infectious chuckle known to American public men, while Roosevelt went off to Africa to shoot big game and carry on the "abundant life" of which he was the apostle.

Taft soon became embroiled in controversies that split his party, especially his conservation policies which were upheld by conservatives and bitterly disputed by the rising Republican progressives. In the mid-term congressional elections, Democrats won the House of Representatives. Republican insurgents moved to block the renomination of Taft, and Roosevelt decided to run against his old friend to save the party from defeat at the next election.

Taft became the regular Republican candidate for the Presidency. Roosevelt left the Republican party to run on the third-party Progressive, or "Bull Moose," ticket.

This split the Republicans and made it practically certain that the next President would be a Democrat. Bryan therefore determined that the candidate of the Party should be a Bryan Democrat and that the time had come for the Party to show it was not merely a pale imitation of the Republican party. Soon he would become the hero of the Baltimore Convention of 1912.

When it opened, Bryan attacked the choice of Alton B. Parker as temporary chairman, and the whole policy of eastern Gold-Standard Democrats. The oppressed people of the South and West, he made it clear, could hope for no relief from a candidate chosen by eastern Democracy; that is, Senator Underwood or Champ Clark. Telegrams poured in from rank-and-file Democrats praising Bryan; an extraordinary manifestation of the care with which voters followed proceedings of the convention.

As it droned along, Bryan made a dramatic move. At an evening session where sat the New York delegation that included Boss Murphy of Tammany Hall, Thomas Fortune Ryan, and August Belmont, he offered the following resolution:

Resolved, That in this crisis in our party's career and in our country's history this convention sends greetings to the people of the United States, and assures them that the party of Jefferson and Jackson is still the champion of popular government and equality before the law. As proof of our fidelity to the people, we hereby declare ourselves opposed to the nomination of any candidate for President who is the representative of or under obligation to J. Pierpont Morgan, August Belmont, or any other member of the privilege-hunting and favor-seeking class.

Be It Further Resolved, That we demand the withdrawal from this convention of any delegate or delegates constituting or representing the above-named interests.

LIBRARY OF CONGRESS COLLECTIONS

Governor Woodrow Wilson of New Jersey and his family in 1912

Governor Wilson is notified
that he is the Democratic nominee
for the Presidency in 1912

LIBRARY OF CONGRESS COLLECTIONS

LIBRARY OF CONGRESS COLLECTIONS

Woodrow Wilson campaigning

There followed a tremendous uproar and Bryan was threatened with physical violence. But he remained calm and his resolution was passed by a vote of more than four to one, and Woodrow Wilson—not Champ Clark, who seemed the sure winner—became the Democratic nominee.

Henry Watterson, the famous Kentucky editor, claimed that Theodore Roosevelt, having built his platform of timber stolen from Bryan's backyard, also used Bryan's tactics.

In 1908, Bryan had asked: "Shall the people rule?"

In 1912, Roosevelt asked: "Are the people fit to govern themselves?"

Roosevelt accused the Republicans of making the wealthy wealthier and merely condescending to let a trickle of treacle drip down to the masses below. And he said that Taft believed there was a class in this country wiser than and above the people, who should govern them.

Here, then, was Theodore Roosevelt making charges against his current opponents, the Republicans, that Democrats had been making against them since Jefferson's day.

Wilson, in speeches of great oratorical power, charged that the government

William Howard Taft
bows out as President as
Woodrow Wilson is inaugurated

LIBRARY OF CONGRESS COLLECTIONS

had long been dominated by industrialists and that the time had come for the "new freedom." It was time to restore competition by destroying tariff protection. It was time to free business and labor from monopoly. It was time to restore hard-pressed farmers and working people to their rightful authority in Washington.

But when Roosevelt was wounded by a maniac, Wilson generously left the stump until he recovered.

Wilson won easily at the polls and the Democrats took control of Congress. In his inaugural address he said there had been more than a mere shift from one party to another in the election. There had been a true change in government.

"The success of a party means little except when the Nation is using that party for a large and definite purpose. No one can mistake the purpose for which the Nation now seems to use the Democratic Party. It seeks to use it to interpret a change in its own plans and point of view . . ."

Wilson looked at the past:

"The great Government we loved has too often been made use of for private and selfish purposes, and those who used it had forgotten the people. . . .

LIBRARY OF CONGRESS COLLECTIONS

Woodrow Wilson in his first term

LIBRARY OF CONGRESS COLLECTIONS

Suffragette tableau in 1913—the ladies got the vote under Wilson in 1919

LIBRARY OF CONGRESS COLLECTIONS

William Jennings Bryan,
a member of Wilson's Cabinet,
plugs votes for women

"Our thought has been, 'Let every man look out for himself...' while we reared giant machinery which made it impossible that any but those who stood at the levers of control should have a chance to look out for themselves...."

What of the future?

"We have made up our minds," Wilson continued, "to square every process of our national life again with the standards we so proudly set up at the beginning and have always carried in our hearts.

"There can be no equality of opportunity... if men and women and children be not shielded in their lives... from the consequence of great industrial and social processes which they cannot alter, control, or singly cope with...."

Wilson delivered his message to Congress in person. Ever since Jefferson, who first sent messages in writing, Presidents had communicated with Congress in that manner.

The Virginia-born Wilson, who had been president of Princeton and progressive governor of New Jersey, in his inaugural address indicted the recent American past and promised a better future. Here were none of the accustomed platitudes of politicians about the glories and immaculate perfections of the

A happy man at the World Series in 1915, with the woman he loved —the widowed President married Mrs. Galt a few weeks later

LIBRARY OF CONGRESS COLLECTIONS

LIBRARY OF CONGRESS COLLECTIONS

LIBRARY OF CONGRESS COLLECTIONS

nation. Instead the speaker turned back to Jackson, Jefferson, Bryan and other men, who believed that the first duty of the Democratic party was to defend the people against the giant forces so often arrayed against them.

Wilson was a profoundly sincere man. His relations with the public were illuminated by an attack he had once made upon hyprocisy in the field of education: "We must believe the things we tell the children."

The President moved, with remarkable success and fidelity, during his first four years of office, to make the principles of the "New Freedom" a reality. The tariff was reduced for the first time since 1861. The nation's banking and credit system was changed and put under public control through the Federal Reserve Act. Under the Farm Loan Act, farmers could borrow money from the government at five or six per cent instead of the ten to twelve per cent they had been paying. The Clayton Act was passed to supplement the Sherman Antitrust Act for the control of big business. The Federal Trade Commission was established to prevent unfair business practices and to enjoin what Wilson called "illicit competition." The Adamson Act set an eight-hour day for railroad workers in interstate commerce. Seamen were benefited by La Follette's Seamen's Act, and Civil Service workers by a compensation law. The positive legislative achievements of the first Wilson Administration had almost no parallel in the nation's history.

But the New Freedom was almost forgotten as the United States entered the First World War, and its gains were partially erased in the drab reaction that followed the war.

22

In 1916 Wilson was renominated by the Democrats whose slogan was, "He kept us out of war." The Republican and Progressive candidate was Charles Evans Hughes, Justice of the Supreme Court.

Hughes straddled the issue of progressivism but Wilson's bold defense of it caused many progressives, including Socialists, single taxers, social scientists, and intellectuals, to enter his camp. Hughes denounced the Adamson Act, establishing the eight-hour day for interstate railroad workers, as a craven surrender by Wilson to the railroad workers. The President replied that the eight-hour day was the goal for which all workers should strive. And when Hughes denounced Democrats for lacking a constructive program, Wilson replied by pointing to a reform program unprecedented in its sweep. The President and the Democratic party in the most straightforward manner espoused their program of reform legislation, and because they did they gained the support of nearly all of the independent progressives, including many who now repudiated Theodore Roosevelt.

But more than domestic issues were discussed in the campaign. There was also the peace issue. Wilson charged that the Republicans were a war party. Hughes' election would therefore mean war with Germany, and the implication was strong that Wilson would keep the country out of war.

When the election returns were in, Wilson had converted the normal Democratic minority into a majority. Eastern centers, where industrial and financial power were located, went for Hughes. But with the almost solid backing of the South and West—regions that had been the backbone of the Jacksonian party—Wilson won with a popular majority of over 600,000 votes. It was a gain for the President of nearly 3,000,000 votes over 1912.

He began his second term as President determined to maintain the technical neutrality of the first thirty months of the conflict in Europe. But on March 27, 1917, word came that the Germans had sunk three American ships in unrestricted submarine warfare. Wilson summoned a special session of Congress and asked for a declaration of war against Germany. On April 6, 1917, the resolution was passed by an overwhelming majority.

This is not the place to recount the complex causes for the decision for war in 1917, or the history of that troubled period. We must content ourselves here with stating that in October 1918 Germany appealed to the President for an armistice, and on November 11, 1918, the fighting ended.

In the November elections for Congress, Republicans won control of the Senate and the House, and although their majority in the Senate was by only one vote, it put control of the Foreign Relations Committee into the hands of the President's enemies.

Wilson nonetheless went to Paris to attend the peace conference and there he won victory only on one major point. His dream of a League of Nations was adopted as an integral part of the peace treaty, and he returned to the United States in February 1919 to fight for ratification of the treaty—including the League Covenant—in the United States Senate.

There were many obstacles to its ratification, including dozens of personal and partisan rivalries and prejudices. There were also factors of decisive importance deeply imbedded in the American tradition. There was no popular belief in 1919 and 1920 that League membership was essential to American security. Who would fight powerful Uncle Sam? Germany was wrecked. Russia was in chaos. One American—or maybe three—could lick fifteen Japanese. So why bother about the future by joining a bothersome League that probably wouldn't amount to more than a *kaffeeklatsch* in any event?

The President decided to carry his fight for the League to the people. It did

THE NATIONAL ARCHIVES

"To make the world safe for democracy,"
President Wilson asked Congress to declare war against Germany

THE NATIONAL ARCHIVES

President Wilson marching in fourth Liberty Loan Parade on Fifth Avenue, New York City

THE NATIONAL ARCHIVES

President and Mrs. Wilson, and Colonel E. M. House

not matter that his health was bad since he had narrowly escaped a stroke in Paris. It did not matter that he was weak and exhausted, and that his physician had told him that a long speaking tour might cost him his life. He went believing that if he took the case to the people they would understand and overturn Senate opposition to the League. During three weeks in September he traveled 8,000 miles in the Middle and Far West and delivered thirty-seven addresses. He got a magnificent reception and the farther west he moved the greater and more enthusiastic were the crowds that greeted him. But the strain of the trip told on him, and he fell prey to blinding headaches.

On September 25, he spoke at Pueblo, Colorado. "It always seems to make it difficult for me to say anything, my fellow citizens, when I think of my clients in this case," he said with tears in his eyes. "My clients are my children; my clients are the next generation. I intend to redeem my pledges to the children; that they shall not be sent . . . to [France]."

After this speech the President, nearing collapse, had to cancel the remaining speeches scheduled and return to Washington. There, in October, he became paralyzed and lingered for days between life and death.

One night during this period, Senator Henry Cabot Lodge, Sr., of Massachusetts, arch Republican enemy of American entry into the League of Nations, dined at the Washington home of Henry Adams. The two men were lifelong friends and their families had been friends for generations. Harold Dean Cater, in *Henry Adams and His Friends,* recounts something of what happened that night at the dinner table of this Adams who was the descendant of two Presidents of the United States and himself a distinguished writer, historian, and scholar.

In the course of the conversation, Senator Lodge became violent in his attacks upon President Wilson. "Suddenly Mr. Adams interrupted the tirade. He brought his fist down on the table and said sharply: 'Cabot.' There was a moment's silence. 'I've never allowed treasonable conversation at this table and I don't propose to allow it now.' "

From the time he was stricken until the end of his term, Wilson was largely confined to his bed, partially paralyzed, embittered. He dealt with the world through a small group that included Mrs. Wilson. In the end, the United States refused to enter the League of Nations. Men have ever since debated whether, given American leadership in the postwar era, the Second World War might have been averted.

There was a strong spiritual resemblance between Woodrow Wilson and his fellow Virginian, Stonewall Jackson, that Old Testament military leader who prayed to the God of Battles before he went out to smite the enemy. Both men were stern and unbending in their Presbyterian resolution. They were stubborn for the right as they saw it, and both died fighting for the right as they knew it.

THE NATIONAL ARCHIVES

Europe welcomed Wilson as a god who would stop wars for all time

Forty centuries of European history looked down on the President of the young American republic

THE NATIONAL ARCHIVES

LIBRARY OF CONGRESS COLLECTIONS

LIBRARY OF CONGRESS COLLECTIONS

LIBRARY OF CONGRESS COLLECTIONS

The three Republicans who led the battle against American entry into the League of Nations

LIBRARY OF CONGRESS COLLECTIONS

The Big Four at the Paris Peace Conference

Wilson on his sixty-fifth birthday

LIBRARY OF CONGRESS COLLECTIONS

THE NATIONAL ARCHIVES

Mr. Wilson's young Assistant Secretary of the Navy at an office party

23

When time came for the elections of 1920, the people were bored with foreign affairs. Senator Lodge, the archenemy of American membership in the League of Nations, may have expressed the prevalent parochialism when he said at the Republican nominating convention: "We must be now and forever for Americanism and Nationalism, and against Internationalism." (One wonders whether he may not have become a whirling dervish in his grave, contemplating the—to him—repulsive spectacle of his grandson, Henry Cabot Lodge, Jr., representing the United States at the United Nations today.)

The idealism of the war years was gone. The world's most mercurial great nation turned its back on the world as though it scarcely existed. It wanted to ride around in Detroit's new cars.

Only a few years before the New York *World* had said: "Financial feudalism died in the United States when Woodrow Wilson took the oath of office as President . . . Mr. Hanna and Mr. Morgan both believed that the country should be governed by property . . . Hannaism died a lingering death, but it died . . . With the election of Woodrow Wilson to the presidency in 1912, the last spark of life had vanished . . . Outside the select circle of Privilege, there were no mourners . . . The new Banking and Currency law has destroyed the conditions under which a Morgan was possible."

And yet . . . at Boston, in May 1920, Senator Warren G. Harding of Ohio spoke to an audience of captains of industry. As sweet water is to the hart at the brook, so were his words to them. "America's present need," he said, "is not heroics but healing; not nostrums but normalcy; not revolution but restoration; . . . not surgery but serenity."

Obviously a man capable of such a combination of balanced phrases, alliteration, and oratorical emptiness, was destined to go far. The speaker became the presidential candidate of the Republicans, with Calvin Coolidge, Governor of Massachusetts, as his Vice-Presidential nominee.

James M. Cox, Governor of Ohio, became Democratic candidate. His running mate was a handsome young New Yorker of patrician ancestry and magnetic personality who had been Assistant Secretary of the Navy during the war. His name was Franklin Delano Roosevelt.

Harding won an overwhelming victory at the polls, and Republicans gained large majorities in Congress.

The record of the Harding régime for fraud and corruption was unparalleled since Grant. Yet the weak, unfortunate, kindly Harding did at least three things that illuminated his generosity of spirit and indicated a certain courage. He pardoned Eugene V. Debs, who had spent three years in jail, and who, while there, had pooled 900,000 votes as Socialist candidate for President in 1920. He persuaded the steel industry to institute the eight-hour day. He defied the American Legion by vetoing the soldiers' bonus bill of 1922.

Greatest of the Harding Administration's scandals were those called "Teapot Dome." Traced to Secretary of the Interior Fall, they involved an attempt to lease government oil lands to private interests in return for large bribes. Fall finally went to jail. He was the first corrupt Cabinet member in American history to receive a just come-uppance.

As Harding prepared for a trip to the West and Alaska early in 1923, he had heard enough about the corruption of his friends—some of them close to him in his Administration—to make him heartsick. "My God, this is a hell of a job," he told William Allen White. "I have no trouble with my enemies . . . But my damned friends, my God-damn friends, White, they're the ones that keep me walking the floor nights!"

Harding died on that trip and was succeeded in the Presidency by Calvin Coolidge.

All was serene in the Coolidge Administration as dishonest leftovers from Harding's day were eliminated, the Republican program bowled along without change, and the nation prospered. Pictured as a cracker-barrel sage, a Yankee "character," Coolidge was becoming a popular President, and was certain of the Republican nomination in 1924.

The Democratic Convention that assembled in New York is notable, not for what it did, but for what it dodged. Evading the prohibition issue, the Democratic platform bravely took a stand for "law enforcement." Dodging the issue of the League of Nations, it adopted an evasive referendum plank. The third issue was the Ku Klux Klan. This violent, brutal, anti-American group had hundreds of thousands of followers, especially in the South and West, whooping it up—behind bedsheets—for religious and racial bigotry. But the nominating convention of the party of Thomas Jefferson and Andrew Jackson did not even mention the Klan. With what contempt the shades of these men must have watched those who desecrated their names!

The Democrats had no courage or convictions of their own. They were merely hydrophobic about Republican corruption. The Harding Administration had indeed been sordidly thievish. Yet since its corruption was great and pervasive, it reflected perhaps the moral apathy of the whole society of the period. Certainly it was unlikely that the people, themselves dripping prosperity, would throw out the Republicans merely because they had been corrupt in office. (As a people, we seem to become stern and indignant about political corruption only during hard times. Then, when there is not enough to go around, we become angered that politicians are stealing hunks of the diminished quantity of bread.) And this seemed the more unlikely when Democrats merely denounced Republicans without offering anything that promised men a better way of life or government.

The Democratic party now stood for nearly nothing. It had neither the courage nor the decency to stand against the Ku Klux Klan, and when its nominating convention met, it was—to its shame—split on this wretched issue. But while the delegates had no courage where courage counted, they were courageous where it took no strength of character to be courageous. They bravely attacked Republican "corruption," monopolies, and lower tariffs, while plumping strongly for a government-owned merchant marine.

The champion of the anti-Klan forces was Alfred E. Smith, the able governor of New York. His name was put in nomination by a spirited man who was crippled by infantile paralysis—Franklin D. Roosevelt. But Smith's Catholicism and his liberalism were hateful to the pro-Klan delegates, and they turned to William Gibbs McAdoo, although he was not one with them in their views.

The balloting went on and on, but neither candidate could command the necessary two-thirds majority, and when the ninetieth ballot had been reached without breaking the deadlock, the delegates turned to other contenders.

Finally, the longest convention in history, on the one hundred-and-third ballot, nominated John W. Davis. A moderately liberal New York lawyer, scarcely to be distinguished in his views and attitudes from a moderately liberal Republican, he had been a Congressman from West Virginia and had served under Woodrow Wilson as Solicitor General. His running mate was Charles W. Bryan, Governor of Nebraska. His chief qualification seemed to be that he was the brother of William Jennings Bryan.

The Republicans, by contrast to the superheated Democratic gathering, nominated Calvin Coolidge on the first ballot, with Charles G. Dawes, a former Chicago banker, as his running mate.

The Republican campaign was pitched on the keynote of "prosperity," and "Keep Cool with Coolidge." The Democrats, for their part, told the country that "A Vote for Coolidge Is a Vote for Chaos." During the campaign, Coolidge conserved his strength and breath by remaining quietly in Washington, saying little.

This time, however, a third party was in the field. The Progressives nominated Robert M. La Follette, the great Wisconsin liberal, whose running mate was Burton K. Wheeler, Democratic Senator from Montana.

The election was a Republican landslide and the Democrats were severely hurt by the Progressives. In California, La Follette polled four times as many popular votes as Davis and twice as many in seventeen other states west of the Mississippi.

The new President stood for little beyond a policy of threadbare meagreness that he put in these words: "I am for economy. After that I am for more economy . . . that is my conception of serving the people."

Mr. Coolidge's inaugural address was the first ever broadcast by radio, and that was its sole distinction. He again aired his piggy-bank mentality as he came out for economy and reduced taxes, and told everybody what they already knew: namely, that the government would play possum for the next four years.

The President sat quietly in the White House thinking his thoughts that he kept to himself, and thriftily banking most of his salary. He permitted nature to take its course in the country and Republican leaders to take their course in the Congress. No one ever had an easier time in the Presidency than Mr. Coolidge. No one in the office ever seemed more aware of what Nietzsche called "the joyful wisdom": a recondite concept that simply means getting out while the getting is good. It was part of Mr. Coolidge's wisdom that he retired in time, whether because his mind told him or his bones told him. And although a volcano had long been smouldering under the White House, he was not even singed by it.

Calvin Coolidge seems always to have yearned wistfully for retrospective political contraception, since if there had been no past there would be no future and hence no tiresome demands for change.

He went back to the Vermont hills and Herbert Hoover, his Secretary of Commerce, whom H. L. Mencken called "a fat Coolidge," became the Republican candidate for the Presidency in the election of 1928. In his acceptance speech he told the nation: "We . . . are nearer to the final triumph over poverty than ever before in the history of the land. The poorhouse is vanishing from among us."

(How could he know that before he left the Presidency, wretched encampments of the impoverished unemployed would be called "Hoovervilles"?) The Republican campaign slogan was: "Let's keep what we've got: Prosperity just didn't happen."

At their convention in Houston, Texas, the Democrats abandoned the cat-and-dog show that they had put on in 1924, and exhibited a high degree of concord. They even had a platform that said something for a change. It pointed out that, under Republican rule, the country's industry was "depressed" and its agriculture was "prostrate." The platform advocated farm relief measures and tariff reform.

Again Franklin Delano Roosevelt placed the name of Governor Smith in nomination, and he concluded with the now famous climax:

"We offer one who has the will to win—who not only deserves success but commands it. Victory is his habit—the happy warrior, Alfred Smith."

The Republicans again ran on a "prosperity" program, but there were other matters of concern in the campaign, spoken and whispered. Prohibition had became a major issue and Hoover was for full enforcement of the Prohibition law (the Eighteenth Amendment to the Constitution), calling it "a great social and economic experiment." Thousands of Democrats were drys, including great numbers of them who annually drank gallons of high-alcohol-content remedies for "sour stomach." But Alfred Smith, without beating about the juniper bushes, came out flatly for modification of Prohibition laws.

BROWN BROTHERS

Al Smith votes for repeal of Prohibition "with delight" as Mrs. Smith (standing) approvingly looks on

Al Smith and friend

BROWN BROTHERS

Al Smith with two good
Democrats from Sardinia

BROWN BROTHERS

There is little doubt that Smith's chances of election were seriously harmed by the fact that he was a Roman Catholic, and although Hoover said that appeals to bigotry "give violence to every instinct I possess," a whispering campaign made many voters believe that a vote for Smith was a vote for the Pope.

Again the Republicans won by a landslide. Mr. Hoover carried Smith's state of New York and five states of the hitherto Solid South.

Now Calvin Coolidge packed his frugal bags and all seemed rosy as he prepared to leave Washington, although he looked sour and his habitual expression was unchanged. William Allen White described it as that of a person "looking down his nose to locate that evil smell which seemed ever to affront him." The fortunate man who got out of town one jump ahead of the tornado, told Congress, just before he took the train, that "no Congress . . . on surveying the state of the nation, has met with a more pleasing prospect than that which appears at the present time."

Mr. Herbert Hoover, who was singularly lacking in imagination, believed that a continuation of Harding-Coolidge policies would make prosperity permanent. ". . . Given a chance to go forward with the policies of the last eight years," he said, "we shall soon . . . be in sight of the day when poverty will be banished from this nation."

But after 1929, as millions became jobless, men were hungry on the farms as well as in the cities, and the American Dream had become a nightmare, people began to wonder why they should go hungry and ill-clad in a country bursting with plenty. As their wonder grew, so grew their indignation, and their distrust of the leadership they had once so fervently admired—the leadership of two cars in every garage, a chicken in every pot, and so forth.

After the spring of 1931, the air became clamorous with choruses of discontent. The Federal Council of the Churches of Christ in America prepared a statement of protest to be read from pulpits. Never before had American capitalism been so corrosively indicted by a group of such impeccable respectability. Then bishops of the Episcopal Church issued a "revolutionary" letter. It demanded that employers abandon the profit motive for the ideal of service to mankind.

The overwhelming majority of the people revolted against the holding action that Hoover favored as the philosopher of prosperity. They wanted a thoroughgoing overhauling of the nation's economic machinery. But even when Hoover moved to help a stricken people, he revealed his curious political theology. Thus Congress in 1930 appropriated $45,000,000 to save the livestock of Arkansas farmers imperiled by drought, and Hoover approved the action. But he opposed an appropriation of $25,000,000 to feed the farmers and their families. This, the President said, was a Red Cross task. In the aftermath, Congress voted $20,000,000 to feed the farmers, but with the proviso inserted, to satisfy the President, that the money should go as a loan rather than as a gift.

Hoover explained that it was morally wrong for the federal government to *give* money for relief. This, he said, "would have injured the spiritual responses of the American people." Then he became noble. "... We are dealing with the intangibles of life and ideals," he continued. "... A voluntary deed is infinitely more precious to our national ideals and spirit than a thousandfold poured from the Treasury."

In Hoover's theology, if government gave a dollar to a hard-pressed farmer, the farmer who took the money was thereby placed in danger of losing his soul at worst, or of having his "spiritual impulses" blunted at best. Yet neither Hoover nor any of his kind had believed that businessmen's souls would be corrupted by government subsidies or Secretary Mellon's lush tax refunds.

The people began to look beyond Hoover as though he were no longer there. They seemed to be fixing their gaze on a New Zion they might attain. There the people themselves—not industrialists and bankers—would make the decisions that affected their daily lives and ultimate fate.

In the election of 1932, President Hoover was again the candidate of his party, while Democrats nominated Franklin Delano Roosevelt, Governor of New York, with John Nance Garner of Texas, Speaker of the House, as his running mate.

The Republican platform devoted itself largely to an attempt to show that the Depression was produced by outside forces, but it contained no mention of constructive plans to conquer it.

LIBRARY OF CONGRESS COLLECTIONS

She turns up every four years

Roosevelt flew to Chicago to accept the nomination in person. There he said: "I pledge you, I pledge myself, to a new deal for the American people . . . This is more than a political campaign; it is a call to arms! Give me your help, not to win votes alone, but to win this crusade to restore America to its own people."

Hoover campaigned vigorously but defensively, telling the unemployed that he would mobilize the nation's resources rather than allow anyone to starve, promising farmers more tariff protection and federal loans, assuring investors of the continuance of the gold standard. He said that everybody would come into fat prosperity if the Republicans won. But he warned that grass would grow "in the streets of a hundred cities, a thousand towns," if Roosevelt were elected.

Roosevelt campaigned confidently although he "overdeclared" himself about economy and a balanced budget. In a campaign speech, speaking of his campaign speeches, he said:

"At Topeka I outlined a complete national plan for the restoration of agriculture to its proper relationship to the nation. At Salt Lake City I outlined a definite program to give us a definite transportation policy, including the rehabilitation of the railroads . . . At Portland I set forth . . . a national policy for the conduct of utilities, and especially those engaged in manufacturing and distributing electric power. At Sioux City I proposed a tariff policy aimed to restore international trade . . . between all nations. At Boston I championed the principle that the national government has a positive duty to see that no citizen shall starve. At Columbus I proposed the protection of the investing public against the evils and fraud perpetrated against them during the past ten years . . ."

On election day—perhaps the most grim election day the country had ever known—forty million voters turned out. Nearly one in three was jobless. Roosevelt swept the nation and his party won staggering majorities in Congress as the revolution of 1932 manifested itself at the polls.

William Allen White, the famous Republican editor-publisher of the Emporia, Kansas, *Gazette,* said that Roosevelt's victory indicated "a firm desire on the part of the American people to use government as an agency for human welfare."

The country could not then know—nor could Roosevelt—that it had elected a President for life.

24

Herbert Hoover was gone. Yet, as events proved, he would not be forgotten—by the Democrats. He ran *for* the Republicans twice. But the Democrats ran *against* him four or five times.

On inauguration day when the banks of forty-seven of the forty-eight states were closed in the financial panic, and a frightened nation wondered what lay

HARRIS AND EWING

The first inaugural—1933

ahead, a hundred thousand people shivered in the crisp Washington air and millions sat glued to their radios to hear the new President.

He began confidently: "This is pre-eminently the time to speak the truth, the whole truth, frankly and boldly."

He continued vibrantly:

"This great nation will endure as it has endured, will revive and will prosper . . . The only thing we have to fear is fear itself. . . ."

The voice went on, full-bodied and confident:

"In such a spirit on my part and on yours we face our common difficulties. They concern, thank God, only material things. Values have shrunken to fantastic levels; taxes have risen; our ability to pay has fallen . . . the withered leaves of industrial enterprise lie on every side; farmers find no markets for their produce; the savings of many years in thousands of families are gone. More important, a host of unemployed citizens face a grim problem of existence, and an equally great number toil with little return. Only a foolish optimist can deny the dark realities of the moment."

The new, untried President of a country gripped by fear, continued:

"The money changers have fled from their high seats in the temple of our civilization. We may now restore that temple to the ancient truths. The measure of the restoration lies in the extent to which we apply social values more noble than mere monetary profit."

If the country needed a new code of ethics in high places, the times also cried out for action, and the President accepted the responsibility of leading the nation out of the wilderness. He said:

"Restoration calls, however, not for changes in ethics alone. This nation asks for action, and action now. Our greatest primary task is to put people to work. . . . I am prepared under my constitutional duty to recommend the measures that a stricken nation in the midst of a stricken world may require."

So began the great Democratic era, 1933–1953.

When Roosevelt came into office the economic machinery of the nation had broken down completely, and the political structure of the country was beginning to fall apart. Those who had nothing—and they were many—wanted at least a minimum of subsistence. Those who had something were frightened lest they lose it. They might have accepted almost anything that would assure their possessions to them. In the words of Arthur S. Link, "So desperate was the crisis on March 4, 1933, and so frightened were congressmen and the people that Roosevelt possessed a power unprecedented in American peacetime history. Had he harbored imperial ambitions, he probably could have obtained dictatorial powers from Congress. Had he been a socialist, he might have collectivized the banks and set the country upon the road to extreme collectivism. However, Roosevelt was neither a fascist, socialist, or Communist. He was simply an old-fashioned American with traditional views on the benefits of the system of private enterprise and ownership of property, who believed that the capitalistic system was worth saving. And the manner in which he and his helpers accomplished this objective revealed the true character of the First New Deal."

The new Administration moved swiftly to attack the Depression. Gone were the days of "business as usual" and "rugged individualism." Congress assembled for its memorable hundred-day session within forty-eight hours after Roosevelt took office. Then there poured out a seemingly endless series of measures attacking the Depression on many fronts and instituting reforms at the same time. Breaking sharply with the concepts of most of his predecessors, Roosevelt believed that the State must take over the economic controls if private individuals failed, and he showed that his administration would not stand idly by while millions of the unemployed suffered.

So swiftly did the Administration move that there did not seem to be enough letters and combinations of letters in the alphabet, as one alphabetic agency followed another: the Federal Emergency Relief Administration (FERA) to

HARRIS AND EWING

Roosevelt and his first Cabinet

Roosevelt at the beginning of his first administration

LIBRARY OF CONGRESS COLLECTIONS

LIBRARY OF CONGRESS COLLECTIONS

The way it looked when Roosevelt took office

LIBRARY OF CONGRESS COLLECTIONS

Youth hopeless in Zion

HARRIS AND EWING

Communion with the people

supply states and local communities with funds to help the jobless; the Civil Works Administration (CWA) to undertake projects to help the destitute during the approaching months of winter; the Works Progress Administration (WPA), the Public Works Administration (PWA), and the National Recovery Act (NRA) to aid industry and its workers.

But it was not only workers who suffered from the Depression. Farmers were everywhere on the verge of rebellion or sunk in hopeless apathy by the spring of 1933. The Administration acted quickly to help them and to stave off revolt on the part of farmers, the most conservative of Americans. For now they were in revolt, not alone against low prices but also against foreclosures of their properties. Committees of farmers threatened to shoot bank or insurance company agents and at foreclosure sales they bought back properties for nominal sums. At Le Mars, Iowa, they went farther. There, in April, 1933, six hundred farmers dragged a foreclosing judge from his bench and beat him into unconsciousness.

In this grave crisis, Congress adopted the Frazier-Lemke Farm Bankruptcy Act, which enabled farmers to recover lost farms on easy terms and, stop-gap measures having been passed, the Administration went on to devise a long-range program for agricultural recovery. Its principal structure was the Agricultural Adjustment Act (the Triple A), the most ambitious agricultural legislation in the nation's history.

As part of the Administration's concern with the plight of fifteen million unemployed and the survival of six million persons who were on city and state relief rolls in the spring of 1933, Congress organized the Civilian Conservation Corps, with an initial grant of $300,000,000. It enrolled 250,000 young men from relief families and set them to work in some 1,500 camps directed by the War Department, on useful projects of reforestation, flood control, and soil conservation. By 1940, when the CCC ended, more than 2,250,000 youths had served in it.

Labor was granted the right to organize—the first time the federal government had endorsed labor's historic aim—under Section 7A of the NRA: "Employees shall have the right to organize and bargain collectively . . . and shall be free from the interference . . . of employers. . . ."

For the multitudes of home owners whose mortgages were in hazard, the Home Owners' Loan Corporation (HOLC) was organized to refinance mortgages, while the Federal Housing Administration (FHA) insured existing mortgages, lent money for repairs of structures, and encouraged the building of new houses with federal financial aid.

Some of the largest businesses of the nation—especially railroads—were in great financial difficulties. Hence the Reconstruction Finance Corporation, organized under Hoover, was enlarged and made huge loans to distressed business enterprises.

Then, turning to protect investors, Congress legislated on banking, finance, and revenue, including a provision for the insurance of bank deposits. Now no depositor—to the extent of $5,000—need fear that bank failure might take his savings, while the Securities Exchange Commission (SEC) sought to eliminate frauds in the issuance of securities to the public.

The First New Deal also organized one of its outstanding and enduring successes in the Tennessee Valley Authority (TVA) with the purpose of flood control and bringing cheap electric power to seven backward Southern states. The National Youth Administration was organized to help young persons between sixteen and twenty-five to secure occupational training and employment, while the Social Security Act provided unemployment and old-age insurance, made benefit payments to dependent mothers and children, and appropriated funds for the public health services.

The First New Deal had been a coalition of workers, farmers and businessmen. But by the summer of 1934 it had begun to disintegrate, and the hate-Roosevelters were already lifting their shrill voices. They had overlooked just one thing. It was not Roosevelt who was the cause of mass discontent, but the terrible suffering that people had endured in the Depression. The conservative revolt flowered in the formation in 1934 of the American Liberty League. It was a combination of conservative lawyers and Democratic politicians led by Alfred E. Smith and John W. Davis—two former Democratic presidential candidates—and big business interests, among which the Du Pont family was the most notable.

They charged that the New Deal was hellbent down the road to communism, and their malice soon made Roosevelt's political struggle with the "economic royalists" intensely personal.

But Roosevelt was far more concerned by rumblings on the left than by cries of alarm on the right. The First New Deal had not brought bright hope to millions among sharecroppers, the unemployed and the indigent elderly, and they appeared to be ready to follow any crackpot who had a bugle.

There was Dr. Clarence E. Townsend, of Long Beach, California, with his Townsend Plan. It proposed that the federal government pay $200 monthly to all unemployed persons over sixty. By 1935 there were thousands of Townsend Clubs and their creator claimed five million followers.

More disturbing was the Reverend Charles E. Coughlin, a Roman Catholic priest in a Detroit suburb. In violently inflammatory radio attacks on the New Deal, he turned his National Union for Social Justice against it and made the wildly exaggerated claim of having nine million supporters.

Still more disturbing was Senator Huey P. Long of Louisiana with his Share Our Wealth Society, his program of making every man a king by giving every family a homestead worth $5,000 and an annual income of $2,500, and confiscating large fortunes as a source of inexhaustible manna for the poor. Long had

The spirit of the New Deal

LIBRARY OF CONGRESS COLLECTIONS

LIBRARY OF CONGRESS COLLECTIONS

LIBRARY OF CONGRESS COLLECTIONS

LIBRARY OF CONGRESS COLLECTIONS

LIBRARY OF CONGRESS COLLECTIONS

become a major leader of mass opinion in great sections of the nation and James A. Farley, in his *Behind the Ballots*, says Democrats were dismayed to learn through a secret poll that "It was easy to conceive a situation whereby Long . . . might have the balance of power in the 1936 election."

Long's attacks upon the wealthy reflected widespread popular opinion. A survey published by *Fortune* in July 1935 found than when men were asked whether they believed the government should allow a man "worth" more than $1,000,000 to keep it, "subject only to present taxes," 45.8 per cent of the persons polled replied in the negative. In the Middle West the percentage replying in the negative rose to 54.6 per cent, and on the Pacific Coast to 54 per cent.

Yet for all that, for all the obstacles and criticisms, and all the mistakes that were made by the First New Deal, the nation was on its way toward recovery when the time came for the nominating conventions.

Republican leaders looking around them saw that the Democratic party was more firmly entrenched than it had been since Jackson's day, and in no hopeful mood they nominated for the Presidency Governor Alfred M. Landon of Kansas. Bereft of ideas, their platform said the New Deal had "dishonored American traditions," but it promised neither revision of its legislation nor anything to take its place.

HARRIS AND EWING

President Roosevelt signing the Social Security Bill

Roosevelt visits Dust Bowl farmers

LIBRARY OF CONGRESS COLLECTIONS

LIBRARY OF CONGRESS COLLECTIONS

Roosevelt brings hope to drouth victims

On the evening of his nomination at Philadelphia, Roosevelt spoke at Franklin Field, filled with a hundred thousand people, while millions of citizens listened on their radios to the warm and resonant voice that seemed to address itself directly to every single listener.

"There is a mysterious cycle in human events," the speaker said. "To some generations much is given. Of other generations much is expected. This generation of Americans has a rendezvous with destiny.

"In this world of ours in other lands there are some people who, in times past, have lived and fought for freedom, and seem to have grown too weary to carry on the fight. They have sold their heritage of freedom for the illusion of a living. They have yielded their democracy."

Roosevelt continued:

"I believe in my heart," he said, "that only our success can stir their ancient hope . . . Here . . . we are waging a great and successful war. It is not alone a war against want and destitution and economic demoralization. It is more than that; it is a war for the survival of democracy. . . ."

America, Roosevelt told the nation, had got rid of the power of royalists in politics. But, he said, "new kingdoms were built upon concentration of control over material things." The old political royalists had been succeeded by "economic royalists," men who derived crushing power from their ability to give or to withhold jobs, to raise prices or lower them, to permit competition or stifle it.

In the campaign of 1936, there was much crossing of party lines. Alfred E. Smith, the once "happy warrior," no longer was happy. He "took a walk" from the Democratic convention and espoused the Republican nominee. Bainbridge Colby, Wilson's Secretary of State, charged that Roosevelt would erase the Constitution. Former Senator Reed of Missouri organized a conference of "Jeffersonian Democrats." It seemed to have no mind at all, for while it denounced Roosevelt it did not genuinely endorse Landon.

Republicans also "took a walk," among them Senator Norris of Nebraska who left his party and received his renomination as an independent. Senator La Follete and Senator Couzens endorsed Roosevelt, while Senator Borah said nothing about supporting Landon.

Roosevelt was then at the height of his popularity but only 36 per cent of the nation's press supported him.

He swept the nation at the election. Only Maine and Vermont were in Landon's column. The people had spoken. More than that, in the election of 1936, as rarely occurs in men's affairs, there had been a close feeling of communion between the masses of the people and their President. Now they had emphatically bid him continue and expand the New Deal program.

In his second inaugural address Roosevelt noted the improvement of the "moral climate of America." He laid down a test of progress: "whether we provide enough for those who have too little." He called attention to "one-third of a nation ill-housed, ill-clad, ill-nourished."

Soon a great storm of controversy would blow over the nation as Roosevelt inaugurated the Battle of the Supreme Court.

In a series of decisions handed down in 1935 and 1936 the Court's majority had nearly paralyzed the executive and legislative branches of the government, and had broken the mainspring of the New Deal. As one authority, A. T. Mason put it, by the early months of 1937 "five willful Supreme Court Justices . . . had in fact contrived well-nigh complete absence of the power to govern." The Court threw overboard such cornerstone New Deal legislation as the NRA and the AAA, the Railroad Retirement Plan, the Bituminous Coal Act, the Municipal Bankruptcy Act, the protection of farm mortgages.

Four of the justices—James C. McReynolds, George Sutherland, Willis Van Deventer, and Pierce Butler—survivals of nineteenth-century Darwinism, were so consistently hostile to progressive legislation that they were called the "Four Horsemen." Midway between the fossils and the progressives were the Chief Justice, Charles Evans Hughes, and Owen J. Roberts, who often voted with the

HARRIS AND EWING

Democrats are singing in the rain
at Roosevelt's second inaugural

"Four Horsemen." There was a small minority of three more progressive justices: Harlan F. Stone, Louis D. Brandeis, Benjamin N. Cardozo.

It appeared certain that the Supreme Court, which had overturned several important New Deal measures, would invalidate the Social Security and Wagner Acts. This would mean the end of the New Deal. In Roosevelt's opinion, "the language and temper of decisions indicated little hope for the future," and if the Court should continue to cast doubts on "the ability of the elected Congress to protect us against catastrophe by meeting squarely our modern social and economic conditions," his administration would signify nothing. And yet there was the mandate thunderously given him by the people on November 3, 1936.

The President felt it was time to act, and in February 1937 he submitted to Congress a judiciary reorganization bill. It empowered him to appoint a new federal judge whenever an incumbent failed to retire within six months after he had reached seventy, but not more than six men could be appointed to the Supreme Court.

LIBRARY OF CONGRESS COLLECTIONS

Roosevelt was stunned by the tremendous outcry that his bill caused. Republicans charged him with ambitions for dictatorship, but he was also opposed by a vigorous opposition within his own party, led by conservative men like Carter Glass of Virginia and Walter F. George of Georgia.

This was a nearly catastrophic rupture and Roosevelt himself must bear much of the responsibility for it. He had not taken Democratic leaders into his confidence before submitting his bill, and he had wielded the patronage stick, through James Farley, too bluntly after the quarrel started. For the first time he lost control of Congress. His chief spokesman in the Senate, Joseph T. Robinson of Arkansas, died when the struggle was hottest. Then the President told the new Senate Majority Leader, Alben W. Barkley of Kentucky, that he would accept a compromise agreeable to all Democrats.

Yet it was not congressional opposition, or public outcry, or Robinson's death, that determined Roosevelt's course. The decisive factor was a sudden and spectacular reversal of attitude by the Court that occurred while the "court-packing" controversy raged, and that suddenly transformed it into a proponent of progressive doctrine.

No one knows precisely why the change occurred, but the conjecture is that Chief Justice Hughes persuaded Justice Roberts to align himself with the pro-

HARRIS AND EWING

Mrs. Roosevelt discussing plans
for a small homes competition

gressives in validating several important reform statutes then being adjudicated. Thus, for example, the Minimum Wage Law of the State of Washington was sustained on March 29, 1937, although a year before, Roberts had joined the "Four Horsemen" to invalidate a similar New York law. Now the Court approved the Washington statute in such a manner as to leave room for nearly any reasonable form of state wages and hours legislation.

In the end, when Roosevelt abandoned the judiciary reorganization bill, he had lost the battle but won the war.

After the Supreme Court had executed its reversal, Roosevelt moved to round out his program. He urged Congress to "extend the frontiers of progress" by establishing minimum wages and maximum hours in industry, and re-establishing the AAA program for farmers. The Fair Labor Standards Act was called by Roosevelt "the most far-reaching, far-sighted program for the benefit of workers ever adopted in this or any other country." The AAA instituted "parity payments" to farmers and was so successful that within a year after its passage, farmers' cash incomes more than doubled.

These two major acts completed the domestic program of the New Deal.

From 1933 to 1936 the health of the American economy slowly improved, but as there came a speculative upsurge in the stock market in the autumn of 1937, the Administration began to behave as though it were frightened of prosperity. Through various fiscal measures it acted to head off what it assumed was a runaway boom in the making; it sharply reduced federal expenditures, and moved to balance the budget by 1939.

The result was a severe slump throughout the economy, and in October 1937 the President called Congress into special session and presented a program to halt the recession and complete the Second New Deal. This program included comprehensive measures to help farmers, legislation to abolish child labor, revision of the antitrust laws, reorganization of the Executive Department. The President expressed his willingness to give business an opportunity to end unemployment by increasing production. "If private enterprise does not respond," he said, "government must take up the slack."

The economic situation, however, grew worse during the winter of 1937–1938, and in April 1938 the President sent a special message to Congress demanding a revision of deficit spending, and calling upon business and labor to unite in a war against the recession. Congress made $3,000,000,000 available to the WPA, a huge public works program was started, bank credits were expanded, and recovery to the near-prosperity level of 1937 was almost complete by the end of 1939.

But soon the Administration's plans for reform and progress would be halted because of ominous developments in Europe and Asia. Roosevelt had sounded a warning to the nation as early as October 1937, after Japan had set up a puppet state in Manchuria, Mussolini had taken Ethiopia, and Hitler had marched into the Rhineland. "It seems to be unfortunately true that the epidemic of world lawlessness is spreading," the President said at Chicago. "When an epidemic of physical disease starts to spread, the community . . . joins in a quarantine of the patients in order to protect the health of the community against the spread of the disease."

The "quarantine speech," however, did not rouse the country, for a firm defense of American interests would require throwing overboard the nation's policy of nonintervention that had been embodied in neutrality legislation from 1935 to 1937. Roosevelt could not rely on his own party because it was badly split on foreign policy. Generally speaking, eastern Democrats were willing to support a stronger foreign policy. Midwestern and western Democrats were opposed to any action that might possibly bring the United States into a second world war. Southern Democrats strongly supported measures for aid to Britain and France, but they were fearful that the Administration's reform measures would upset race relations in their communities.

The President's difficulties were further increased by the Congressional elections in November. Republicans made huge gains in Congress and became a strong power for the first time since 1932. The President had to be careful not to drive any Democrats into alliance with the Republicans, especially southerners whose support was vital to him.

In his annual message to the Seventy-sixth Congress on January 4, 1939, the President devoted himself largely to an exposition of the dangers of the totalitarian threat to religion, democracy, and international peace. In domestic affairs, he asked for no reform legislation, but requested that deficit spending be continued until full recovery had been assured.

Then, in effect, he announced the end of the great reform movement of the Second New Deal. He said: "We have now passed the period of internal conflict in launching our program of social reform. Our full energies may now be released to invigorate the processes of recovery in order to preserve our reforms."

What was the New Deal? What judgment shall be passed upon the elements that went into it? Was it radical or conservative? Perhaps the best answer to these questions comes from Franklin D. Roosevelt.

"As a Nation we have rejected any revolutionary program," he said in 1938. "For a permanent correction of grave weaknesses in our economic system we have relied on new applications of old democratic processes." American history confirms this judgment. The New Deal was essentially conservative in character. It stemmed from long decades of discussion and experience, and some of the concepts it employed had come from Republican proposals as well as Democratic.

25

As the nominating conventions met for the election of 1940, domestic issues receded into the background. Life-and-death issues faced the nation. Would America enter the war? Would it come to the aid of Britain? Would it fight Hitler? The fate, not only of the United States, but of the world hung upon the answers to these questions.

The Republican convention met two days after the fall of France, but no one would have known that the democratic world was in jeopardy by a reading of the thisaway-thataway platform it adopted. It pledged the country to "Americanism, preparedness and peace." The democratic victims of aggression were promised "such aid as shall not be in violation of international law or inconsistent with the requirements of our own national defense."

The convention chose as Republican nominee for the Presidency, Wendell L. Willkie, a utilities executive and successful corporation lawyer.

It was not until the middle of May, after Hitler had overrun the Low Countries and France, that Roosevelt decided to run again. He was defying one of the oldest and most sacred tabus in American constitutional practice, the limitation of a President to two terms in office. This tradition, dating back to Jefferson, was now challenged by Roosevelt. But, for all his popularity, it is unlikely that the

LIBRARY OF CONGRESS COLLECTIONS

LIBRARY OF CONGRESS COLLECTIONS

My friends . . .

HARRIS AND EWING

HARRIS AND EWING

The third inaugural

LIBRARY OF CONGRESS COLLECTIONS

HARRIS AND EWING

Children, Santa Claus and friend

U. S. ARMY PHOTOGRAPH

President Franklin D. Roosevelt and Mr. and Mrs. Harry Hopkins, with daughter, listening to the Army Band and carol singing at the White House, Christmas Day, 1942

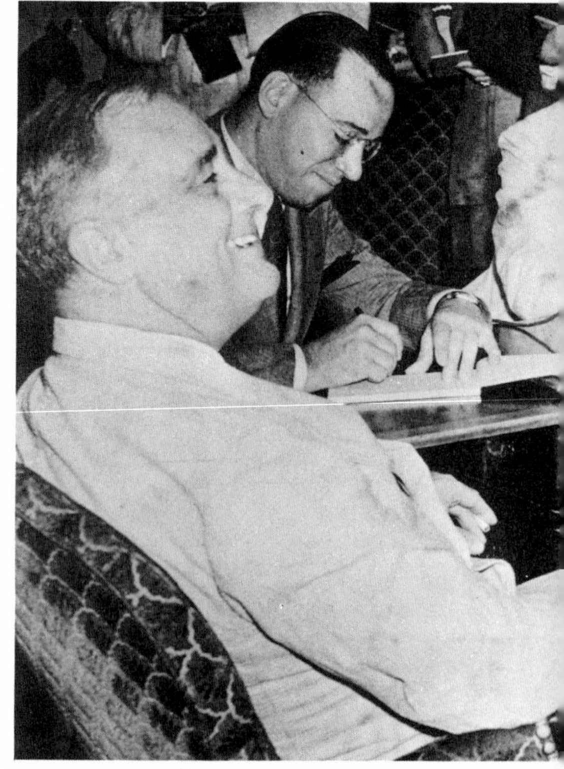

Press conference

HARRIS AND EWING

THE NATIONAL ARCHIVES

Franklin D. Roosevelt, 1942

tradition could have been overthrown if it had not been for the great and increasing emergency of the war.

"Hitler's triumphs," wrote D. W. Brogan, "were one of the most powerful forces making for the acceptance of the breach of the tradition . . . Hammering on the sacredness of the tradition and attempts to scare the voters by threats of an American dictatorship were of little moment compared with what was seen, by millions, as a threat from a German dictatorship . . . Those Americans who were frightened of Roosevelt and Hitler were more frightened of Hitler. Those who were not frightened of Hitler were nearly all against Roosevelt anyway. How many times did one hear the remark, 'Well, I'm really opposed to the idea of a third term for any man but with such a madman loose in Europe, it becomes necessary to keep a trained . . . man at the helm.' The third term argument cost the President some votes . . . But . . . not as many voted against . . . Roosevelt on grounds of the third term as might have been expected under the circumstances."

The President was immensely popular and strong within his party. Yet he had to force down the throats of the nominating delegates his choice for Vice-President, Henry A. Wallace, Secretary of Agriculture.

In a strange campaign between two men who were in basic agreement upon many great matters such as aid to Britain, Roosevelt became the nation's first third-term President. (Also its last, since a constitutional amendment now limits the President to two terms.) The people disbelieved Republican claims that he would become a dictator if elected. They ignored similar charges made by Herbert Hoover. Nor did they pay the slightest attention to newspapers that hysterically warned that a Roosevelt victory would end free American elections.

In the 1940 campaign Roosevelt, Willkie, and their party platforms promised aid to countries fighting the Axis. Both men also promised that they would not take the country into war. "Our national policy," said Roosevelt, "is not directed toward war. Its sole purpose is to keep war away from our country." At the same time he called the United States "the great arsenal of democracy," and said that "no combination of dictators could weaken the American resolve to help Britain."

HARRIS AND EWING

The President asks Congress for a declaration of war against Germany and Japan

LIBRARY OF CONGRESS COLLECTIONS

During 1940 and 1941 the President fostered measures that flouted neutrality. These included the trade of fifty destroyers to Britain for naval bases, the Lend-Lease Act, and the construction of a naval base in Northern Ireland. After hostilities had taken place in September 1941 between a German submarine and an American destroyer, Roosevelt said in a Navy Day speech that "America had been attacked," and "the shooting war had started." The country was indeed engaged in undeclared naval warfare, yet the nation's refusal to engage in all-out warfare made it impossible to use its resources efficiently.

But with Pearl Harbor in December 1941, the nation embarked on total warfare with the Axis, political hostilities were laid aside temporarily, and the people united behind the President as the country entered the Second World War. Never since the dark days of the Revolution, nearly one hundred and fifty years before, had it confronted so grave a military menace or undertaken a task so staggering.

Congressional leaders look on as President Roosevelt signs the bill which declared the United States to be in a state of war with the Japanese Empire: The White House, Washington, D. C., December 8, 1941

U. S. ARMY PHOTOGRAPH

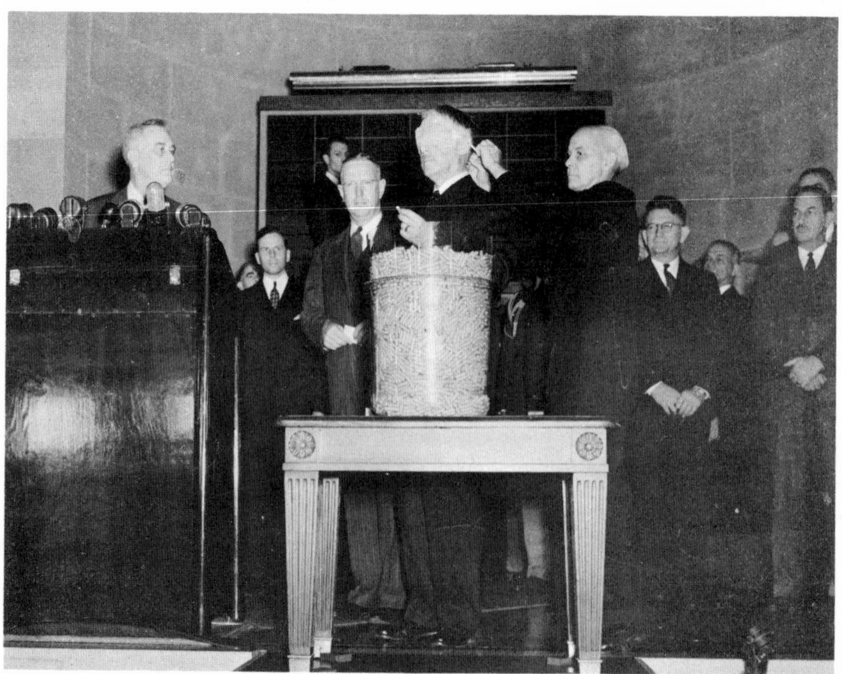

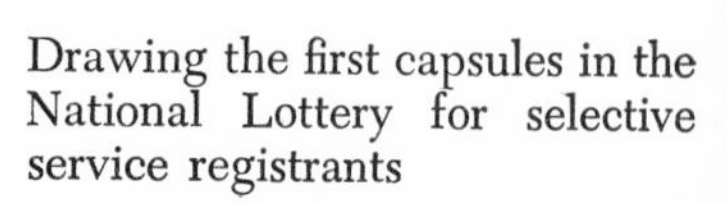

Drawing the first capsules in the National Lottery for selective service registrants

U. S. ARMY PHOTOGRAPH

Servicemen and friend

HARRIS AND EWING

President Roosevelt
and his Secretary of State

U. S. ARMY PHOTOGRAPH

U. S. ARMY PHOTOGRAPH

The President talks
to shipyard workers
during the war

U. S. ARMY PHOTOGRAPH

Roosevelt visits Casablanca and has an army lunch
with Generals Clark and Patton and Harry Hopkins

U. S. ARMY PHOTOGRAPH

The Commander-in-Chief visits American troops in North Africa

Cairo Conference leaders: Generalissimo Chiang Kai-shek, President Roosevelt, Prime Minister Winston Churchill, and Madame Chiang Kai-shek pose informally for photographers in a garden near the Mena House, November 25, 1943

U. S. ARMY PHOTOGRAPH

At home, the President was successful in bringing Democrats and Republicans together in a common effort. The parties worked smoothly together in prosecuting the war, while even on domestic issues party lines were frequently blurred. But the future began to take on another aspect during the congressional campaign of 1942. Then the Republicans made such large gains that their victory in 1944 seemed feasible, a prospect made seemingly the more reasonable of attainment by the election of Thomas Dewey as the first Republican Governor of New York since 1920.

All this, as the aftermath proved, was more of a conservative upsurge than merely a strong Republican revival. When the Seventy-eighth Congress met in January 1943, many Southern Democrats joined with Republicans to form a majority coalition dedicated to seizing control of legislative policy from the Administration, destroying certain parts of the New Deal, and letting the President know that Congress, like the flag in *The Star-Spangled Banner,* was "still there."

Republicans nominated Governor Dewey for the Presidency, with Governor John W. Bricker of Ohio as his running mate.

Many Democratic conservatives furiously resented Roosevelt's leadership and yearned for an aged-in-the-wood conservative leader. The President let them stew and fret as to his fourth-term intentions, waiting until a week before the Democratic convention to say that he would accept the nomination if offered him. "All that is within me," he wrote, "cries out to go back to my home on the Hudson River... But as a good soldier... I will accept and serve."

Roosevelt was promptly nominated but a bitter struggle arose over the nomination for the Vice-Presidency. Henry Wallace was strongly opposed by city bosses, southerners, and many moderates who thought that he was temperamentally unfitted for the Presidency and lacked qualities of political leadership. The President did not insist upon the choice of Wallace. It fell, with his approbation, to Harry S. Truman, Senator from Missouri. "Who the hell is Harry Truman?" Admiral William D. Leahy asked when Roosevelt told him of the vice-presidential nominee in the summer of 1944.

As Dewey campaigned, the Allies were winning great victories everywhere, the home front was economically stable, and men were reluctant to change governments in the midst of a world crisis. Yet there was the ever-recurring argument of the condition of Roosevelt's health, while Democrats were deeply worried because the President seemed to take little interest in the campaign.

But in a speech before the Teamsters' Union in Washington on September 23, millions again realized that Roosevelt was the master campaigner, and he followed this speech with others in New York City, Wilmington, Delaware, Chicago, and New England.

Before the teamsters, Roosevelt began mockingly:

"Well, here we are together again—after four years—and what years they have been! I am actually four years older, which seems to annoy some people. In fact, millions of us are more than eleven years older than when we started in to clear up the mess that was dumped in our laps in 1933."

He derided Republicans who "suddenly discover" every four years just before election day that they love labor, when they had been attacking labor "for three years and six months."

Finally, in a memorable and famous passage, he set the nation to laughing as he talked about his dog Fala. "... Republican leaders," he said, "have not been content with attacks upon me, or my wife, or my sons—they now include my little dog, Fala. Unlike the members of my family, he resents this. Being a Scottie, as soon as he learned that the Republican fiction writers had concocted a story that I had left him behind on an Aleutian island and had sent a destroyer back to find him at a cost to the taxpayers of two or three or twenty million dollars, his Scotch soul was furious. He has not been the same dog since."

Pollsters predicted a very close election, but when the returns were in Roosevelt had won a smashing victory, receiving 432 electoral votes to Dewey's 99.

Roosevelt ordained an inaugural of the utmost simplicity since he did not deem it a time for joyous celebration when Americans were dying on battlefields, and he made a brief address of only 573 words. "Today in this year of war 1945," he said, "we have learned lessons—at a fearful cost—and we shall profit by them. We

LIBRARY OF CONGRESS COLLECTIONS

The first and last fourth-term President campaigns for the last time

U. S. ARMY PHOTOGRAPH

The two old friends conferring at Yalta

have learned that we cannot live alone, at peace; that our own well-being is dependent upon the well-being of other nations far away..."

In February Roosevelt went to the Crimea to meet with Stalin and Churchill, and on March 1, the end of the war being in sight, he appeared before Congress. Haggard and exhausted, for the first time he alluded publicly to his infirmity when he apologized for delivering his report on the Yalta conference from a chair. He said: "I know that you will realize it makes it a lot easier for me in not having to carry about ten pounds of steel on the bottom of my legs."

Six weeks later, Franklin D. Roosevelt was dead.

U. S. ARMY PHOTOGRAPH

Marshal Stalin has a dinner party at Yalta

The President reports to Congress on Yalta

HARRIS AND EWING

U. S. ARMY PHOTOGRAPH

Roosevelt is dead

Free men everywhere mourn Roosevelt's death

U. S. ARMY PHOTOGRAPH

U. S. ARMY PHOTOGRAPH

Salute to the dead Commander-in-Chief

The gentlemen discuss political strategy

HARRIS AND EWING

26

On the evening of April 12, 1945, Harry S. Truman took the oath of President from Chief Justice Harlan F. Stone.

The next morning he told newspapermen: "I feel as though the moon and all the stars and all the planets have fallen upon me. Please, boys, give me your prayers. I need them very much."

When the new President took office, the war was rapidly approaching its end. Allied armies were in Germany, American forces were preparing to invade Japan, and now, in April, the United Nations Conference opened in San Francisco with forty-six nations in attendance.

In mid-July Truman met with Churchill and Stalin in Potsdam, and in August the war ended with the surrender of Japan.

Although the nation then faced grave problems abroad, and at home was confronted with the difficult task of converting the economy from a war to a peace footing, such was the impatience of the people that little, apparently, could be done quickly enough. "The rush to disarm late in 1945," wrote Walter Millis, "was surely one of the most expensive economies—in terms of life and effort as well as money—in which the United States ever indulged." Yet nothing could stop the country's headlong—and headless—rush toward "normalcy," and Truman was even blamed for not moving faster.

Mr. Truman
becomes Vice-President

HARRIS AND EWING

HARRIS AND EWING

Mr. Truman becomes President on the death of Franklin D. Roosevelt

HARRIS AND EWING

The President's
first press conference—
"Pray for me, boys"

HARRIS AND EWING

The President announces
Germany's unconditional surrender

U. S. ARMY PHOTOGRAPH

Triple handshake in Potsdam

The country had built within an unprecedentedly brief time the mightiest fighting force men had ever known. Now it proceeded to wreck it with even greater speed and a reckless disregard of consequences. A limited demobilization of the army began in 1945, and with the collapse of Japan all the armed services began sending men home as quickly as possible. But in January 1946 there were riots among servicemen abroad and frenzied protests at home because demobilization was not moving speedily enough. Soon the greatest fighting forces of all time were reduced to dimensions meagre in relation to the country's international responsibilities. By midsummer of 1946 the great wartime Army and Navy numbered only 1,500,000 and 700,000 men, respectively.

It did not matter that time after time in 1946 and onward until the Korean War, the President and his military advisers told the country that its armed strength was barely enough to meet the country's minimum international responsibilities, much less to provide security against aggression. Congress was hell-bent for economy and in 1949 the President and his new Secretary of Defense, Louis Johnson, joined them. The result was that by the spring of 1950 American armed strength had been brought to a postwar low.

On the eve of the Korean War Congress imposed a $13,000,000,000 ceiling on defense expenditures and reduced the Army to 600,000 men—ten active divisions.

During 1944 and 1945 the country was obsessed with fears of a postwar economic depression that might bring national bankruptcy and international chaos. Yet the government's wartime success in mobilizing industry and labor set some men thinking along bold lines and caused them to reject what they regarded as the outmoded concept of "boom and bust." Thus, for example, Henry Wallace and CIO spokesmen talked of "full employment," of "60,000,000 jobs," and of mobilizing the resources of government to achieve this aim. The promise of "full employment" had indeed been a major Democratic pledge in Roosevelt's campaign of 1944, and it was reaffirmed by President Truman in the summer of 1945.

In the spring of 1946 poison ivy grew amid the jonquils of Washington as a sulphurous battle occurred in Congress over the removal of price controls. Soon after the Japanese surrender the Office of Price Administration (OPA) announced that it would gradually relax wartime controls over prices, wages, and scarce commodities. It did end the rationing of most things during the last months of 1945 and the first months of 1946, and it held the general cost of living to an increase of 3 per cent. But the floodwaters of inflation were battering against the dikes of control. Consumers with billions in their pockets were frantically buying in black markets. Organized labor was out for higher wages. Farmers had joined Republican leaders to demand an end to controls.

In the spring of 1946, Truman vetoed a watered-down price control bill that extended the life of the OPA for one year, and price controls went out of the

HARRIS AND EWING

The country's best-known pedestrian

window on July 1. Then as Congress debated what to do, prices soared like a runaway balloon and the nation was faced with its severest inflation since 1942; and while consumers cussed, Republicans played up the theme of Democratic confusion and ineptitude concerning price control. But there was worse to come. When price controls on meat were restored in August, farmers kept their cows at home and embattled housewives bid up the price of nonexistent hamburger. This was bad for the Democrats. For as everybody knows, a housewife who cannot get hamburger is more dangerous than Medea wronged.

By this time everybody was sore at the President, including organized labor. It was sore because of his manhandling of John L. Lewis and his stern action in breaking the railroad strike in 1946. Conservatives were sore at him because he had fought vigorously for welfare and civil rights legislation. New Dealers were sore over two incidents that threatened a bad split in the Democratic party in 1946. The first was the resignation of Harold Ickes as Secretary of the Interior, in a row over the appointment of Edwin Pauley as Undersecretary of the Navy. The second was the firing by Truman of Henry A. Wallace, his Secretary of Commerce, because he attacked the Administration's increasing resistance to Russian demands.

All these grievances the Republicans warmed up and presented under the telling slogan, "Had enough?"

As mid-term elections approached in 1946, polls noted that the President's "popularity," which had stood at 90 per cent when he took office, was down to 30 per cent.

To the surprise of no one, Republicans won control of Congress for the first time since 1930.

Mr. Truman and the Republican-dominated Eightieth Congress co-operated remarkably on foreign policy. But they fought a constant battle over domestic measures having to do with taxes, civil rights, housing, and farming. All of them would figure in the extraordinary election of 1948.

Truman asks Congress for aid to Greece

HARRIS AND EWING

HARRIS AND EWING

The Greek people express their gratitude to the President

HARRIS AND EWING

The President signs the great North Atlantic Pact Bill

Triple play by three Democrats

U. S. ARMY PHOTOGRAPH

Berlin airlift—one of Truman's bold decisions in foreign affairs

Berlin airlift—a great city is kept alive by air

U. S. ARMY PHOTOGRAPH

Never during the preceding twenty years had Republicans been so confident of taking over the government as during the early months of 1948. Nonetheless they looked for a sure-fire winner and rejected as candidate Governor Harold E. Stassen of Minnesota, and Senator Robert A. Taft. They turned to the war hero, General Dwight D. Eisenhower, who was still in service. The General, however, refused to run on the ground that military men ought to stick to the military. He said:

"I am not available for and could not accept the nomination... The necessary and wise subordination of the military to civil power will be best sustained when life-long professional soldiers abstain from seeking high political office."

Republican chances of victory appeared the greater as Democrats engaged in civil war. Henry Wallace tried to enlist New Dealers in a program of collectivization and opposition to the resistance of the Truman Administration to Soviet imperialism. He became the third-party candidate for the Presidency on a Progressive Citizens of America ticket, and many observers believed that he would destroy Democratic chances of success in 1948 by polling from five to eight million votes.

No one seemed to want Truman as presidential candidate, or to have any confidence in his ability to win, except one man. His name was Harry S. Truman. Democratic progressives tried to avoid having to choose between Truman and Wallace. Thus, Americans for Democratic Action first tried to force Truman to go back to Independence, Missouri. This failing, the group sought to find a winner in the person of Justice William O. Douglas or General Eisenhower.

On the score of Truman's alleged incompetence as a President and his inability to be re-elected, intellectuals such as the ADA, and city bosses, were one. Frank Hague of Jersey City, Jacob Arvey of Chicago, Edward Flynn of New York, joined the movement to oust Truman and draft Eisenhower.

Then, as though this were not enough to smash the Party, southern Democrats, infuriated by Truman's civil rights program, threatened to "take a walk" if the convention should adopt a strong civil rights plank.

Sometimes the behavior of the Democratic party is reminiscent of what Samuel Butler said in another context: "More effort has been made to keep together that artificial collection called the human family, than any other institution."

The so-called "Dixiecrats" met at Birmingham, waved Confederate flags, formed the States' Rights Democratic party, and nominated Governor J. Strom Thurmond of South Carolina and Governor Fielding L. Wright of Mississippi on their "national" ticket. They won control of the Democratic party in Alabama, Mississippi, South Carolina, Louisiana. But they failed in their major objective. It was to organize an all-southern rebellion and use it to throw the presidential election into the House of Representatives where they could wield the balance of power.

With the right and left wings of the Party in rebellion, it was a gloomy, squabbling Democratic convention that met in Philadelphia. There was a great row over the civil rights plank but the convention adopted one of some strength. Whereupon the entire Mississippi delegation and half of Alabama's—thirty-five men in all—left the convention. Those who remained felt apparently that while they might miss the departing brethren, they could get along without them.

The convention finally nominated Truman not because it wanted to, or because it had not tried to avoid it, but for the compulsive reason that it had no one else to nominate. The President chose Senator Barkley of Kentucky as his running mate after Justice Douglas had declined to run.

Truman had waited for hours to appear before the convention. At last he stood in the presence of the harassed, reluctant, dispirited men who had nominated him. It was then two in the morning.

The speaker brought with him a magic of confidence and courage and vitality that quickly banished the funeral-home atmosphere of the convention hall. "Senator Barkley and I will win this election," he cried. "We'll do that because they're wrong and we're right . . . and I'm convinced it [the Democratic party] will be elected a fifth time next November . . . The people know that the Democratic party is the people's party, and the Republican party is the party of special interests. . . ."

By now ten thousand people were on their feet cheering wildly, and they continued to cheer as the courageous little man on the platform first described Democratic achievements in restoring national prosperity and then angrily, emotionally, listed shortcomings of the "do-nothing Republican Eightieth Congress."

Most of those who heard Truman had neither affection for him nor admiration. But they could not fail to sense his courage, his profound belief in himself and in the principles of his party, and as he went on they knew inwardly that they were listening to the fightingest presidential acceptance speech since the days of William Jennings Bryan.

The President ended with the surprising statement that "On the twenty-sixth day of July, which out in Missouri they call Turnip Day, I'm going to call that Congress back. . . ."

Then he announced his plan:

"I'm going to ask them to pass laws halting prices and to meet the housing crisis . . . to act on aid to education . . . ; a national health program, civil rights legislation . . . ; and increase the minimum wage . . . ; an adequate and decent law for displaced persons in place of the anti-Semitic, anti-Catholic law which this Eightieth Congress passed."

Truman would test Republicans at the special session of Congress and the "American people will decide on the record."

Even long before the Democratic convention, many newspapers, columnists, and press associations had buried the Democratic party. Walter Lippmann, for example, gave it a magisterial funeral:

"The country may say to the Democrats as they relinquish the power they have held so long and the heavy responsibility they have borne through dangerous days, 'Hail and farewell . . . We shall meet again.' "

Clare Boothe Luce, lady keynoter at the Republican convention, and a Philadelphic oracle in a Christian Dior dress, said that President Truman was "a gone goose," whose "time is short and whose situation is hopeless."

Governor Dewey, the Republican nominee, had no doubt of the accuracy of the lady's vision.

When President Truman addressed the joint session of Congress, he asked for "strong, positive action" to check inflation and to secure better housing, federal aid to education, a national minimum wage and expansion of social security, civil rights legislation, a comprehensive health insurance plan, a long-range farm program, a reciprocal trade agreement act, and approval of the St. Lawrence Seaway treaty.

Senator Taft said the President's recommendations were an "omnibus left-wing program," and Republican leaders agreed to adjourn Congress as soon as possible while doing as little as possible.

Truman took his fight to the people, and especially to the farmers of the Middle West. He denounced "gluttons of privilege" who, he said, were putting up "fabulous sums of money" to beat him. He said that "the do-nothing Republican Eightieth Congress" had "stuck a pitchfork in the farmer's back," and that the power lobby, operating through Congress, had "crudely and wickedly" cheated the people.

Wherever he went he encountered almost solid opposition from the polls and the press, but was greeted by friendly and often enthusiastic crowds. The people were willing to listen to the small, folksy man from Independence, Missouri.

Dewey made the same speech over and over. It was to the effect that only the Republican party and a Republican President could take care of the nation's affairs in a troubled world abroad and assure it of prosperity and reduced taxes at home. He doused this prune whip with liberal doses of soothing syrup. Mr. Truman called his opponent's speeches "mealy-mouthed." Perhaps Mr. Dewey could afford to be smug and complacent. Had he not been assured by the nation's press, pollsters and "experts" that he would inevitably become the next President of the United States?

On election night, Truman went to bed confident and serene. He woke to find that he was President in his own right. The people had elected him. They had also given Democratic control of Congress. Gerald W. Johnson came close to the heart of the mystery of democracy—and of the election—when he wrote of

HARRIS AND EWING

Mr. Truman, Miss Truman, and Senator Barkley beginning the 1948 campaign

LIBRARY OF CONGRESS COLLECTIONS

One of the few men who believed that Truman could be elected President in 1948

INTERNATIONAL NEWS PHOTOS

U. S. ARMY PHOTOGRAPH

Spontaneous welcome
for the new President

U. S. ARMY PHOTOGRAPH

Inauguration Day—January 20, 1948

Truman in the reviewing stand at the inaugural parade after he had taken the oath of office at the Capitol:

"Mr. Truman stands there," Johnson said, "not in his own right, but as representing you and me and Joe Doakes down the street, and Martha, his wife, and the kids playing baseball in a vacant lot. He represents a Negro and a Jew and an American-born Japanese. In reality, it is a Minnesota farmer taking the salute, a Georgia cracker, a Pittsburgh steelworker, a New York girl filing clerk, in whose honor the bombers darken the sky over Washington. . . .

"This is more vividly apparent in the case of Mr. Truman than in that of most Presidents; for his election is due to the fact that the common man took matters in his own hands . . . He is conspicuously the common man's choice . . .

"The common man must make good, or incur the scorn of his enemies and plunge his friends into despair . . . If the democracy of America cannot master the existing crisis, it is idle to look for another; if we fail, tyranny must overwhelm the world. . . ."

27

In his annual message to Congress on January 20, 1949, Truman launched what he called the Fair Deal, while in subsequent messages to Congress and appeals to the nation he repeated his proposals and sought to bring them into a broad, cohesive program.

He got less than he asked of the Eighty-first Congress. But he also got more than many men thought he could get from it.

Truman got amendments to the Social Security Act that brought ten million new beneficiaries into the system, secured passage of the Housing Act of 1949, and obtained large sums for slum clearance and construction of houses for low-income families.

But the Administration did not win repeal of the Taft-Hartley Act, a major objective of organized labor. It failed to secure adoption of its program for agriculture—the Brannan Plan. Its proposal for national health insurance was defeated, and it did not get far with its program of civil rights.

Yet Truman won increased appropriations for the TVA, the Rural Electrification Administration (REA), and the Farmer's Home Administration, an agency that lent money to farmers for rehabilitation and farm purchase. And in June 1950 the President gained approval of a displaced persons bill to admit some 400,000 European refugees and replace the "anti-Semitic and anti-Catholic" measure of 1948.

There was an interval of about eighteen months between the beginning of Truman's second term and the outbreak of the Korean War. The wonder is that in this period the Fair Deal obtained so much progressive legislation. For this was a time of prosperity and relative contentment when men merely wanted to enjoy what they had and were little concerned with planning for the morrow.

It is impossible here to do little more than mention some of the important acts of the Truman Administration in foreign affairs. For boldness and sweep they are perhaps without precedent in the long line of the American presidency.

In the spring of 1947 the Administration determined upon a change in foreign policy that has stood the test of these dangerous times and which remains, with some variations, the cornerstone of the nation's foreign policy today. Growing impatient of arriving at friendly accommodation with Soviet Russia, the Administration undertook a bold program designed to halt further expansion of Soviet power in Europe, the so-called Truman Doctrine of containment.

Its first great expression was the Greek-Turkish aid bill in 1947. It won the support of a Republican Congress. Now the United States had made a new departure in foreign policy and served notice by the passage of this bill that henceforth, to deny further strategic advantages to Russia, it would aid nations and governments that resisted Soviet pressure and penetration.

Toward the end of December 1947 the President submitted the draft of an economic cooperation bill (the Marshall Plan) calling for seventeen billion dollars in aid during the next four years, and earnest debate on it soon began. It opened in the Senate on March 1, 1948, with an address by Senator Vandenberg that brought senators and spectators to their feet in applause. "The greatest nation on earth either justifies or loses its leadership," he said. "We must choose . . . The iron curtain must not come to the rims of the Atlantic either by aggression or by default."

The Marshall Plan, as is well known, was a principal factor in preventing Russian-dominated communism from taking over some of the great countries of western Europe.

So successful indeed was the Marshall Plan that beginning in April 1948 the Kremlin set out to thwart it and to prevent the unification of Germany by establishing a blockade of Berlin, then under four-power control but isolated in the eastern zone of Germany. Allied withdrawal from Berlin in the face of superior enemy force would have destroyed Allied influence in Germany, and brought a tremendous diplomatic victory to the Soviet Union that would have resounded throughout the world.

It never occurred to Truman to retreat. When military leaders raised the question of withdrawal on June 28, the President said, "We are going to stay." It was decided to supply West Berlin by air and thereby force the Russians to make the choice of peace or war, and from June 1948 to mid-May of 1949 the United States and British air forces accomplished the miracle of carrying and delivering 2,500,000 tons of supplies and keeping a large city going from the air. Finally, the Russians yielded and lifted the blockade.

As the first great step toward Atlantic unity was the Marshall Plan, the second was the conclusion of the North Atlantic Pact, a military alliance that created a counterweight to Soviet power in Western Europe; it reflected American determination to protect that area against Soviet attack, looked forward to the creation of joint military forces, and brought within its purview the United States, Canada, Britain, France, Italy, Portugal, the Netherlands, Belgium, Luxembourg, Denmark, Norway, and Iceland.

When the United States intervened in the Korean War, the Republican leaders, Governor Thomas E. Dewey and John Foster Dulles, were thoroughly approving of the action. In the Congress, members of the House stood and cheered on June 28, 1950, when they learned that President Truman had ordered air and naval forces to defend South Korea. Nor was this all. Senator Taft said

Korea, 1951

U. S. ARMY PHOTOGRAPH

he would vote for a resolution authorizing the use of United States forces in Korea, even though he opposed the President's acting without congressional approval.

Yet the summer and autumn of 1950 were seasons of fear and crisis in the United States and the nation was convulsed by a congressional campaign of almost unprecedented bitterness. Republican spokesmen did not clearly repudiate United States intervention in Korea, but they did say that blunders by Truman and Dean Acheson, his Secretary of State, had made the Korean War inevitable. All this was incidental to the Republican charge that communists had infiltrated the Administration and especially the State Department. No one exploited the nation's fears of communism more skillfully or more ruthlessly than Representative Richard Nixon of California in his successful election to the Senate.

Democrats retained control of Congress by a narrow margin in the elections of November 1950. But they had meaningful results that portended bad times for Democrats. The agrarian Middle West again became Republican. Communism and inflation had proved to be popular issues that could be exploited more fully in the future, and to these were added charges of corruption on the part of some figures in the Truman Administration. Yet it was the country's participation in the Korean War that caused the greatest discontent. Though nearly every American had cheered when Truman intervened in Korea, the country was swept by disillusionment and despair when the Chinese came into the war and Truman refused to take desperate measures that might have quickly put an end to the fighting.

It seemed certain that the Administration and the Democratic party would be engulfed in a flood of peace sentiment.

28

The small man with the sad, shrewd face, and gentle eyes, looked out upon a serried mass of men and women whose ranks extended from floor level to galleries high under the lofty roof. Television cameras upon him, he began to speak to the thousands within his presence and to the millions of Americans who listened in their houses and places of assembly. For this was a quadrennial year —1952—when the nation chooses its President for the next term.

The speaker was chairman of the Democratic National Convention. He was also Speaker of the House of Representatives and had served longer in this great office than any man in the nation's history. Sam Rayburn spoke and these are some of the things he said about the Democratic party.

"... I do *not* say that the Democratic party is all-wise. I do *not* say that it is all-knowing. I do *not* say that it is all-holy. For this would not only be untrue, but it would be to attribute to men what is of God alone.

"Yet I do say that the Democratic party is merciful, it is humane, it is compassionate. If it should ever cease to possess these qualities, it would cease to be the Democratic party, and ought to be condemned to oblivion."

The speaker compared men and parties:

"... As every man is the sum total of his inheritance, environment, and experience, so are political parties. Some men will instinctively oppose injustice, whether or not it directly concerns them. Some men are selfless and some are selfish ... And in every case, when the chips are down, they will behave according to the laws of their inner natures.

"All this is a matter of heart ... The Democratic party may not always have been wise, but it has always had a good heart. And when a man or a political party has a good heart, you know that he or it will never let you down."

This leads to certain consequences politically:

"... Even if the Republican platform promised you heaven on earth, there would still remain what counts most—the interpretation and administration of it.

Thus, Chief Justice Charles Evans Hughes once said "The law [the Constitution] is what the Supreme Court says it is.' The law, then, is not merely the statute as written. It is the statute as interpreted by the courts. So, too, a political platform or expression of creed is what the party making it interprets it to be. And how does a party interpret a program? It does it in the only way it can do it. By its inner light, its instinctive feelings, its habits of thinking acquired through many decades.

"Hence you must ask yourselves whether the record of the Republican party, its ambitions, its habits of thinking, its qualities of thought, are such that it would interpret its platform broadly for the many, or narrowly for the few. . . ."

Mr. Rayburn then made one of his rare personal allusions to his own life, to explain why, in part, he was a Democrat:

"An underdog in my youth on a back-country Texas farm, the absorbing interest of my life has been underdogs . . . That is why, when I go home to my little town of Bonham, Texas, and see farmers' cars parked in the courthouse square, while the men visit their friends and the women shop . . . my heart is gladdened.

"For when I was a child and lived 'way out in the country, I'd sit on the fence on Sundays and wish to God that somebody would ride by on a horse or drive by in a buggy—just anything to relieve my loneliness. Loneliness consumes people. That's why I'm glad to see farmers have cars. That's why I want America's children of today and tomorrow to have a more plenteous and joyful childhood than I had. That's one of the reasons why I've been a lifelong Democrat. And that is also why, when the country chose us for the task in the first administration of Franklin D. Roosevelt, we Democrats began to remake this nation in the name of *all* the people."

Mr. Rayburn, the Democrat, sees man plain and sees him whole:

"The Democratic party recognizes that man is a three-fold creature. First, he is of God. Second, he is a social being. Third, he is an economic being. In order to be a whole man, in order to be harmonious with God and the world, a man must be all three of these things.

"The Democratic party looks upon man, not as a statistic, but as a spiritual being; a living, pulsing, willing, hoping, creature of flesh and blood. It regards neighborliness as next to godliness. For my neighbor comforts me in my distress and he shares his bread with me and he takes me by the hand when I am lost in the wilderness."

The speaker made it clear that the Democratic party was no enemy of change. "The Constitution," he said, "is not a straitjacket . . . Changing times and changing concepts have moved the American people . . . to amend it twenty-two times. If not all change is good change, not to change at all is to be dead; or, worse, to be dead while still living. . . ."

Under Roosevelt and Truman, change had been so great that it was tanta-

Four Democrats, including Speaker Sam Rayburn, at their ease in Texas

mount to a bloodless revolution. And now Mr. Rayburn turned, as all Democrats must turn, to Thomas Jefferson:

"Thomas Jefferson said, 'I certainly am not an advocate for frequent and untried change in laws and constitutions . . . But I know also, that laws and institutions must go hand in hand with the progress of the human mind.

" 'As that progress becomes more developed, more enlightened, as new discoveries are made, new truths are disclosed, and manners and opinions change with the change of circumstances, institutions must advance also, and keep pace with the times. . . .' "

Mr. Rayburn applied this Jeffersonian concept to the Democratic party in his time:

"The promises and performances of the Roosevelt and Truman Administrations are not only in accord with the spirit of our great institutions and traditions but they are also of a piece with the oldest aspirations of the nation, beginning with 'life, liberty and the pursuit of happiness.' They were, and they are, an experiment in promoting the greatest good of the greatest number. If that be wrong, then we are wrong. . . ."

HARRIS AND EWING

HARRIS AND EWING

The candidate, Senator Paul Douglas and Steve Mitchell

In the election of 1952, the Republicans chose as their presidential candidate General Dwight D. Eisenhower, with Senator Richard Nixon of California as his running mate.

The Democrats turned to Adlai E. Stevenson, Governor of Illinois, and through a genuine "draft"—one of the rare instances of the rarest of political maneuvers—called upon him to run for the Presidency with Senator John Sparkman of Alabama as vice-presidential candidate.

Governor Stevenson welcomed the delegates to Chicago. But he made no conventional, perfunctory speech that men usually hear upon such an occasion. Instead, the wise, mirthful, sad, and soaring words of the speaker who was little known to most of his audience, profoundly impressed them, while many of them felt that shock of revelation which comes when the speaker lifts the listener out of the workaday world onto a plateau where the rarefied air stimulates the mind and the long view fills the heart with exaltation.

Here, moreover, was a politician who scorned one of the weapons of his profession—evasion. "Where we have erred," he said, "let there be no denial; where we have wronged the public trust, let there be no excuses. Self-criticism is the secret weapon of democracy, and candor and confession are good for the political soul. But we will never appease; we will never apologize for our leadership in the great events of this critical century from Woodrow Wilson to Harry Truman!"

The speaker turned to first principles:

"What counts now," he said, "is not just what we are against, but what we are for. Who leads us is less important than what leads us—what convictions, what courage, what faith—win or lose. A man doesn't save a century, or a civilization, but a militant party wedded to a principle can."

Here was a man who employed wit and humor as they had not been employed by a public man since Abraham Lincoln. Speaking of the Republican nominating convention lately held in Chicago he said: ". . . For almost a week pompous phrases marched over this landscape in search of an idea, and the only idea they found was that the two great decades of progress in peace, victory in war, and bold leadership in this anxious hour were the misbegotten spawn of bungling, corruption, socialism, mismanagement, waste and worse. . . .

"After listening to our misdeeds awhile I was surprised the next morning when the mail was delivered on time! Our friends were out of patience, out of sorts and, need I add, out of office."

In his speech of acceptance, Adlai Stevenson told the delegates:

"I have not sought the honor you have done me . . . I would not seek your nomination for the Presidency because the burdens of that office stagger the imagination. Its potential for good or evil now and in the years of our lives smothers exultation and converts vanity to prayer."

A profoundly religious man in the widest sense of the term, the speaker continued:

"I have asked the merciful Father, the Father to us all, to let this cup pass from me. But from such dread responsibility one does not shrink in fear, in self-interest or in false humility.

"So, 'If this cup may not pass from me, except I drink it, Thy will be done.' "

The Democrats, under the leadership of Adlai E. Stevenson, conducted a campaign notably free of demagoguery, appeals to prejudice, or promises of pie in the sky. Stevenson, a Jeffersonian rationalist, used the language of reason as he addressed the nation, and the most careful examination of his campaign speeches yields no cargo of the base metal that so often is pawned off in political campaigns for sound coin of the realm.

In the end, the people chose as their next President, Dwight D. Eisenhower, and the Democratic succession that stretched back to 1932 was for the moment halted.

INDEX

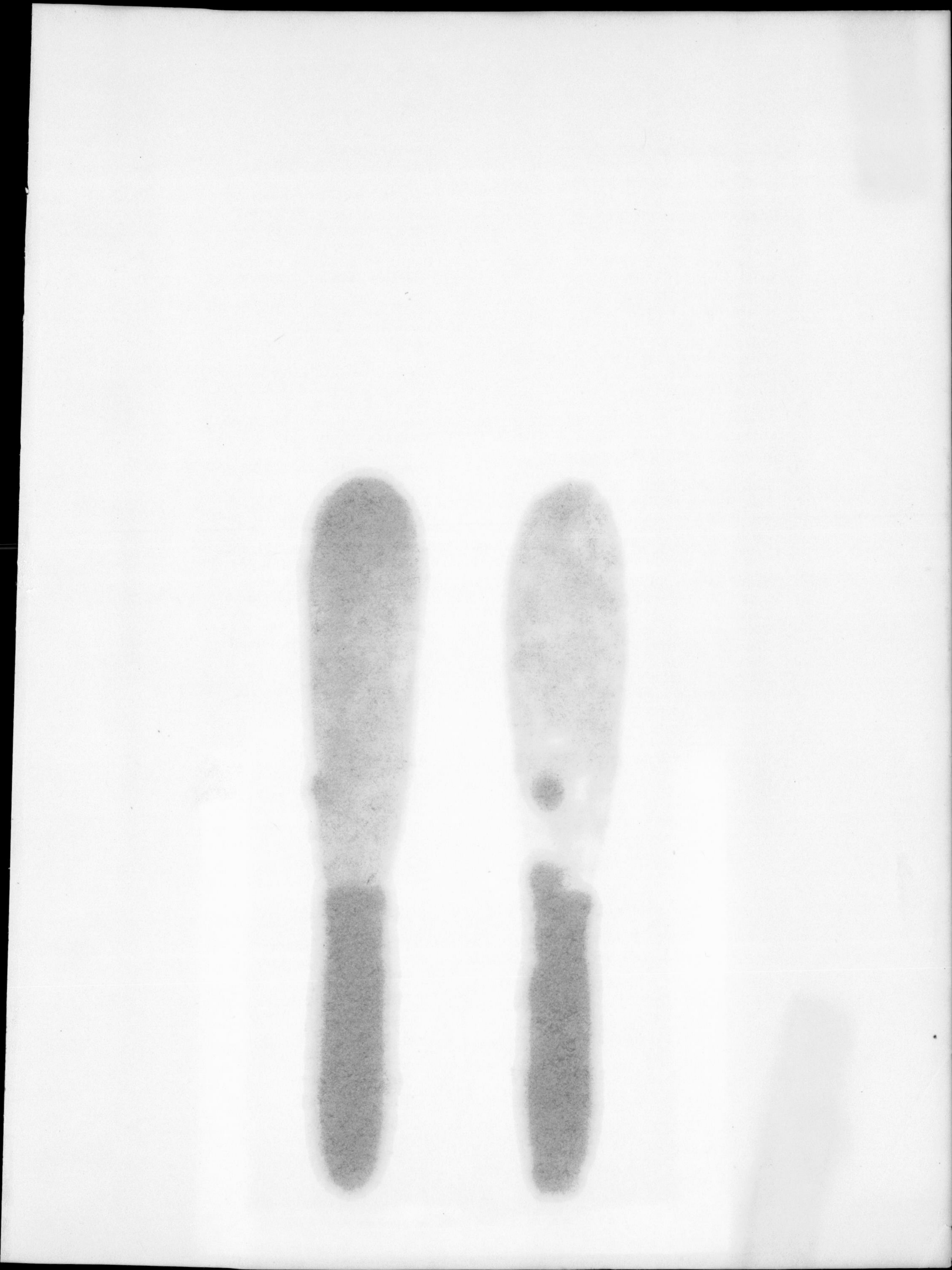